# HAPPINESS in
# OVERLOOKED
# MIRACLES

# HAPPINESS in OVERLOOKED MIRACLES

*Orlando, Fl, USA September, 2020*

## DR. ENG. FAHIM JAUHARY

## HAPPINESS IN OVERLOOKED MIRACLES
## ORLANDO, FL, USA SEPTEMBER, 2020

*iUniverse books may be ordered through booksellers or by contacting:*

*iUniverse*
*1663 Liberty Drive*
*Bloomington, IN 47403*
*www.iuniverse.com*
*844-349-9409*

*Because of the dynamic nature of the Internet, any web addresses or links contained in this book may have changed since publication and may no longer be valid. The views expressed in this work are solely those of the author and do not necessarily reflect the views of the publisher, and the publisher hereby disclaims any responsibility for them.*

*Any people depicted in stock imagery provided by Getty Images are models, and such images are being used for illustrative purposes only. Certain stock imagery © Getty Images.*

*ISBN: 978-1-6632-1846-9 (sc)*
*ISBN: 978-1-6632-1847-6 (e)*

*Library of Congress Control Number: 2021902859*

*Print information available on the last page.*

*iUniverse rev. date: 02/11/2021*

## Word of thanks & gratitude

When we reach what we dream of, we must remember those who contributed to our arrival and supported us, with a word of thanks, the constant talk of the Messenger of God (peace be upon him): "God does not thank those who do not thank people."

So I would like here to express my love and gratitude to my wife, who has always stood by me in the development of this book, and has provided me with her ideas and thoughts of the Qur'an.

I also thank my daughters and my sons, who have strongly supported me for writing this book, and have also contributed to their opinions and the treatment of the text.

Dr. Fahim Jauhary

# CONTENTS

# INTRODUCTION

Before the advent of Islam in the world, ignorance was widespread, human values were almost non-existent. Slavery was one of the common axioms among nations, the strong were killing the weak, the method of son shopping and prostitution was widespread, and female infanticide habits were widespread among the poor, in addition to other inhumane ethics.

Islam came and in less than about 40 years, one of the largest ruling states in history has been built with Islam as its religion, a Muslim state was built with its borders from the Mediterranean to India. Thrones fell from countries that had dominated the region for thousands of years. The reason is that Prophet Mohammad and his honorable companions (the Sahaba) addressed the nations in the words of God, with the Holy Quran in word and deed. The Sahaba had high intellectual Maturity and they benefited from the Wisdom of Prophet Mohammad. What does the Qur'an say, what are Mind purification and intellectual Maturity and what is Wisdom? God said:

"Our lord sends amongst them a Messenger of their own, who shall rehearse Thy Signs and Wisdom, and sanctify them: For Thou art the Exalted in Might, the Wise" (Albaqara verse129)

For this holy Qur'an, which is sent by God for all people, an influence on the minds of those who understand and think? I see people whose language is not Arabic from east and west, they became Muslims or at least respect Islam when they understand what is written in Quran. Their understanding of Islam is stronger and deeper than some people who claim Islam, or those who hide their religion in front of others. That is not for anything but because Islam does not need preciosity, nor to the sermons and appearances. Islam needs a conscious mind and an honest self with itself. But here I respect and do not deny what many of our distinguished scholars do in clarifying the thoughts of the Holy Quran, and their dedication to traveling around the world to educate God's servants about the heavenly message. God preserved the holy Quran for the worlds, as He descended upon Our Lord Muhammad, God said:

"We have, without doubt, descended the Massage, and we will assuredly guard it" (Alhijr 9).

Then the Quran is an original compilation and the final verbal avowal from God to our prophet and the mankind. Quran is a masterpiece of immense literary value, it is a continuation and a completion to tasks assigned to the prophets Abraham....Moss and Jesus, Quran has a wealth of information- both worldly wisdom and intellectual conceptions, that provides the code of life for all mankind. God said:

"The Messenger believes in what was revealed to him from his Lord, as do the men of faith. Each one (of them) believes in God, His angels, His Books, and His messengers (Mohammad, Jesus Christos, Moses..... peace be upon them): "We make no distinction (they say) between any of His messengers." And they say, "We hear and we obey. (we seek) Your forgiveness, our Lord, and to You is the destiny." "God does not burden any soul beyond its capacity. To its credit is what it earns, and against it is what it commits. "Our Lord, do not condemn us if we forget or fall into error. Our Lord, do not burden us as You have burdened those before us. Our Lord, do not lay on us a burden greater than we have strength to bear. Blot out our sins, and grant us forgiveness. Have mercy on us. You are our protector; help us against those who stand against faith". (Al Bakara verse.285, 286).

Why do not we address the world with Wisdom included in the Quran?

It is a mission for whom God has granted the privilege of wandering in his possession, and God will hold us accountable if we fail to carry this message.

Therefore, I went on to write this brief note Book, hoping that it would be helpful for Muslims and non-Muslims in understanding the thoughts of the Quran as I understood them. The Qur'an contains a huge amount of material miracles, overlooked or forgotten, including spiritual miracles that are at the heart of our material life. And to feel the effect of this understanding on the person himself, as I felt about my life, whereas present generations believe in the tangibles, not in impalpable or metaphysical. They have no time to deliver into the sermons and interpretations of our ancestors. That is why the topics of this note included the importance of the Maturity of man to understand common sense and the importance of knowledge, which leads to Wisdom. Maturity, knowledge, and Wisdom are the most important tools of persuasion and dealing with people, as well as I talk about the Structure of man; physical and spirituality, then the definition of Faith, Belief, Will, Desire, and their relationship to human Habits, building the personality of human and determining his destiny. Also, I included in this book some Meditations about the Doctrine of Reality and Laws of life, as well as the attempt to clarify some of the scientific miracles of the Qur'an and its effects, in addition to the concept of Slavery and Extravagance.

Someone said: "Reading a book is thinking about using someone's mind".

It is my duty here to admit that all that is said in this book is an attempt to be subject to the rule of diligence and in the possibility of right and wrong, and God knows everything.

I hope from God that I have succeeded in what I intended, for my jealousy of Islam.

Dr.Eng. Fahim N.Jauhary

# 1

## WHO AM I?

When I was in the elementary classes, my father- God's mercy on him - was telling me that I should become a huge palace or a huge building and that every day of my life is a stone in this building. Thus Before sleeping, I had to ask myself what new information I added to this building, and when the building is completed and I live in it, I will be happy. So I had to always seek knowledge because Knowledge gives happiness. My father did not find, in his childhood, a father who directs him to knowledge, the same as his colleagues in his era who became ministers and important figures.

During my elementary school, the teacher warns us from the fire of hell and from the torment of the grave and the like, and what follows, if we made a mistake in reading a verse from the Qur'an, whose meaning we did not understand at the time... but I finally saved it by heart ... my family celebrated that occasion: a taxi tour around the city, topped by a decked and decorated chair. All of this did not help in getting to knowledge of God for me.

From a young age I have been searching for knowledge, Science knowledge, knowledge of the matter, knowledge of creatures, knowledge of philosophy, knowledge of God, does He exist? Where is He? How do we know? How do we think? ... I was and still curious to learn and know how everything works. I did not find an answer in my childhood ... I am certain that knowledge gives us happiness. So I have been reading a lot of books and periodicals.

My days went as well as any ambitious creature is going to know, I finished school and worked as an employee to provide money for my university studies, after I got a doctorate in technical engineering and worked as a researcher and teaching assistant at the university, I focused on reading books of natural sciences, philosophy, psychology, administration, and others, in order to understand different ideas for different people, as well as the stories of great people in history, and I have sought to find answers to my perplexing questions from what the thinkers wrote in German, English and Arabic languages. I am still curious, I'm trying to know.

As a result and through knowledge, I am proud that I am a Muslim. Islam came to the whole world with a logical philosophy, so I am universal, as prophet Mohammad said: "There is no virtue for an Arab over a Non-Arab or a white man over a black man except by piety". The world is my homeland, and the land of God is wide.

Islam has established rules and laws for this life and the afterlife, these laws of life are made by God the life creator. Many laws for everything, Are we aware of them, and do we think deeply about them??

# 2

## PERCEPTION & MATURATION

**There are two aspects of human maturity: Mental maturity and Personal maturity:** "Maturity is the ability to respond to the environment decently". A person's thoughts change as he gets older; his view changes to many things and becomes more mature. Maturity stems from human's environment around them that teaches them, from the vision or insight that God granted to human and from his awareness, his sensory, mental, and scientific awareness, God says:

"It is He who has created for you hearing, sight, and hearts (heart's vision): little thanks it is ye give" (Almo'menoon verse. 78).

Sensory perception or **feeling** - hearing, vision, fumbling in addition to fumbling by heart – are the beginning of the stage of perception in human beings, followed by mental perception, then scientific perception ... and if we deny **feeling**, we deny perception and deny maturation.... The Almighty says about false believers:

"Fain they deceive Allah and those who believe, but they only deceive themselves, and realize it not" (Albakara 9).

God also says:

"….Truly it is not their eyes that are blind, but their hearts which are in their breasts" (Alhaj 46).

This means that, God abolished the first sense of feeling from the heart's vision, so it does not become that they had mental awareness or a scientific awareness of God Almighty's existence (Sheikh Al-Shaarawi)[16],

"Nay, man will be insight against himself, even though he was to put up his excuses". (Alqiama 14, 15)

"Now, Insights (Proofs) have come to you, from your Lord, if any will see, it will be for his own soul, if any will be blind, it will be to his own (harm)…." (Alana'am 104).

**Perception** [5] is from Clairvoyance (insight) and it is the beginning of change for the better, it is the beginning of growth and development. **Without the Clairvoyance, man would have lived in a loss like animals.**

It is natural that the conscious mind actualized with its senses, realizes what it lacks in science and learning, then comes the role of the unconscious mind that stores the outcome Perception to use it when needed[6], and here comes the role of Maturity.

As for maturity, it is the completion of experience and wisdom in matters of life. Maturity is the ability of a person to distinguish between what is right and what is not right, between good and evil, between what benefits and does not benefit, between how I live happily or becomes naughty. Maturity is not with a person from his birth. Maturity gives a person the concept of life, how he behaves and thinks about various things.

The growth of a person is considered the first and indispensable stage of maturity, but intellectual maturity is not related to age, so the age of a mature person is just a number. Maturity is an endless intellectual station.

Among the characteristics of a mature person are the following:

1 - The mature person forgives at his ability and pays the harm with good deeds. God said: "…Repel (Evil) with what is better. Then will he between whom and thee was hatred become as it were thy friend and intimate…." (Fussilat 34)

2 - To know when to speak and when not to speak.

3 - The mature person adapts quickly to a changing, non-ideal world to find the best because he neglects the lost and takes the present.

4 - He is always optimistic, satisfied with what God destined for him.

5 - The mature person understands the causes of others' behavior towards him.

6 - He respects himself and assumes responsibility for what is happening to him, and admits his mistake, while the immature person always accuses the circumstances and others in his lack of success, he is always complaining, while the mature one works on reform and change.

7 - The mature person knows himself, his capabilities, and what he wants in life. Therefore, he builds his future within the limits of his capabilities and does not wait for coincidences.

8 - The mature person does not get excited by calamities or charity.

9 - Maturity is when we begin to understand the small things before we talk about the big ones.

10 - The mature person is not easily critical of the news, but rather examines it to know what is behind it, and can question the validity of the information before believing it.

11 - The mature person is aware of the value of things, not advertising, and trademarks.

12 - The mature person is happy to talk to strangers and to know everything new.

13 - The mature person maintains good relations and mastered withdrawing from harmful relationships and failed friends.

14 - The mature person gives because he wants it, he does not want emotion from anyone.

15 - A mature adult loves to travel and he enjoys his life without caution, he enjoys increasing his knowledge of the world and people's.

16 - The mature person leaves the argument even if he is sure of his opinion.

17 - The mature one has no authority or meaning of others' judgment on him.

18 - The mature person loves knowledge and reading.

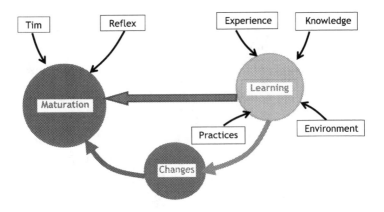

# 3

# WISDOM

**Wisdom** as psychologists [40] has defined it is the **"integration of deep understanding, knowledge, and experience, which includes tolerance towards uncertainty in life".** Wisdom is an important element of the human personality that combines many characteristics; namely experience, knowledge and intelligence that is in a wise person. Some have also defined wisdom as the science in which we look for the truths of things, as they are in existence as much as the human brain can absorb it. Also, wisdom is the right thing to say and act, which is to infect the right to science and reason, because it is the right mental opinion. Or it is that a human being with insight into many things.

The virtue of wisdom in the Holy Qur'an: Almighty said:

"He granteth wisdom to whom He pleaseth; and he to whom wisdom is granted receiveth indeed a benefit overflowing, but none will grasp the Massage but men of understanding" (Albaqara 269).

Prophet Mohammad said: "There is no envy except in two: a man whom God gave him money, as he uses it on the right, and a man who God gave him wisdom, as he judges with it and teaches it."

Our Lord Jesus Christos (poh) said: "Wisdom is the light of every heart."

Scholars [43] have studied the concept of wisdom since ancient times, 450 B.C., the Greek thinker, and philosopher Aristotle said: "Wisdom is the head of science, literature, and art; it is the inoculation of understanding and the results of minds." As his classical mathematics teacher, Plato said: "The four virtues are wisdom, justice, courage, and moderation". Also from the rule of Socrates, the wise teacher of Plato and the founder of Western philosophy, said much more: "Diseases without medicine: lack of religion and lack of literature, "no virtue without knowledge", "Minds of talents and science gains", "who is stingy on himself is less to the others", "Great woman is the one who teaches us how to love".

"Socrates has been asked: Why have you been chosen to be the wisest of the wise men in Greece? He replied: "Maybe because I'm the only man who admits he doesn't know."

The German philosopher Jog Wilhelm Hegel [44] defines wisdom as the highest possible level of man, after knowledge in man is complete and history reaches its peak, then wisdom is born in man. Wisdom is the next and last stage of philosophy; it is the climax of the peak and the ends, congratulations to those who reach wisdom and sobriety.

Wisdom gives man a great creation, gives him a sense of balance, and generates awareness of how events are handled, and wisdom is required in various matters of life, for good and bad, because it has several qualities required, such as calmness and poise at the time of calamities, namely looking at things in a deeper way to look at the causes of the problem and its complications and find possible solutions to it.

Wisdom is one of the attributes of the prophets, apostles, and righteous. God said to our prophet Muhammad: "You are a great creation."

Wisdom is also the qualities of those who think about creating heavens and earth from scientists. Wisdom helps man to be right in his words and actions, so he's standing and honor among those around him rise. With wisdom, the human mind is complete and becoming loved by those around him, enjoying its opinions.

So who is a wise person? Al-Hakim or a wise man is a reasonable person who likely put decisions to righteousness, because of his life experience. But it is not necessary for anyone who has experience in his life to be wise. One of the qualities of Al-Hakim is that he is always optimistic about the ability to solve most of the problems of his life, he is optimistic in the darkest situations, he is calm and careful when faced with difficult decisions, and he uses his sense and intelligence to draw important points in the vision of the merits of things. Psychologist Igor Grossman [39] says that: wisdom is associated with positive effects on human life, and this reduces his negative feelings, and also says that "a wise person has a relatively long life and has good social relationships.

A wise person is characterized by a set of qualities [42.41], including:

1) the ability to analyze and draw lessons from his knowledge and experiences in his field of specialization, and here age is not considered a factor" but maturity is essential.

2) To be honest, neutral in his judgment, unmoved by his desires, vanity and self-love does not meet with wisdom.

3) Wise persons look at things positively and realistically, even constantly criticizing themselves.

4) The wise man thinks quietly before he speaks, the word that comes out of the tongue will not return.

5) Al-Hakim understands others and works as an investigator, he has no bad or a good person, he understands the reasons for the actions of others, understands their justifications, to give his best advice.

6) The wise person accepts others as they are without changing their actions, may they accept his ideas.

So to be wise in your opinions, you have to manage all the experiences of your life and extract from it the wisdom of its occurrence, and extract causes and results. You should look at your life experiences in social, emotional, scientific, and cognitive processes. That turns your experiences into pearls of wisdom. Everything we go through is not a coincidence or luck, but it is destined for you from within or outside your will. If you understand it you will advance your mind and understanding of things, and you will be able to give the right judgment to what is around you. Wisdom is the juice of life experiences, a wealth of all kinds of accidents and anecdotes, and inspiration afterthought works and gets things done. You will be convinced that your life experiences would have informed you of a conscious understanding of everything that surrounds you.

# 4

## HUMAN STATE

The Human being at any time and place is a standing state itself, as it is any country of this world [17]. It has its eras, changing places, and multiple climates. God created the human being from seven elements: the **Mind**, the **Self**, the **Character**, the **Body**, the **Spirit**, the **Clairvoyance** (insight), and the **Instinct** (Commonsense). Then God ordered Humans to use their mind, according to their time and place, in a way that does not contradict with one of the **firm and constants in the Shari'ah** (main Islamic Laws). Also God's order the virtue, i.e. what is recognized as one of the good things permitted in his era, for the continuity of a decent life.

The human being, then, is a sovereign state. The **Self** dwells in the **Body** and then tastes death and exits it. The Almighty said:

"...And if thou could see how wicked are in the dark of death, and the angels stretch forth their hands, saying: yield up yourselves out today..." (Alan'am 93).

The Self in the body is the ruler. In the human body, the Self is governed by the physical laws of the body. The Mind is the general manager and the body is the people, the constitution of this state is the Character, which is politicized by the Self ... The Character controls the Mind, and the Mind in turn orders the tools of the body such as the hand, eye, tongue, etc. ... by making voluntary movements to do something, and these tools have no right to rebel against the mind. Some minds are nice to the body because they know certainly that they have a common interest. But other minds do not take into account what will happen to their body, because they are minds ruled by stupid or bad personalities. As for involuntary movements of the body such as blood circulation, breathing, appetite for food and sex, it is the specialty of Instinct.

The puzzling question here is: Do other creatures such as birds and animals have the Self?

God said: "There is not an animal that lives on the earth, nor a being that flies with its wings, but nations like you. Nothing have We omitted from the Book, and they all shall be gathered to their Lord in the end" (Al-Anam 38).

I may understand from this verse that when creatures die they will return on the Day of Resurrection so they have Selves in their bodies, and they return on the Day of Resurrection, but do not be held accountable because God did not give them the freedom of will. And as long as they have Selves, then they have Character or personality that serves as a fixed constitution for their life. But God knows better.

So, to control our body, first, we refine our Character: wisdom, love of others, goodness, forgiveness, and sincerity at work are good qualities of Character, which in turn create a good life.

But false pride, enmity, hateful, hatred, foolishness, envy, cunning, and laziness are qualities of bad Character, which destroy life and create unhappiness for man and those around him.

God said:

"Nor can goodness and Evil be equal, Repel (Evil) with what is better. Then will he between whom and thee was hatred become as it were thy friend and intimate. And no one is granted such goodness except those who exercise patience and self-restraint, none but persons of the greatest good fortune." (Fusilat 34-35).

Here the verse urges us to forgive and to be patient in distress.

God said:

"So that ye may not despair over matters that pass you by, nor exult over favors bestowed upon you. For Allah loveth not any vainglorious boaster." (Alhaded 23).

This verse calls on man to rely on God and be patient with what has happened to him and warns us against false pride.

God said:

"And from the mischief of the envious one as he practices envy"

(Alfalak5).

Envy is an evil that has an impact on the envious, but God protects the believer from envy.

God said:

"Satan plans is to excite enmity and hatred between you, with intoxicants and gambling, and hinder you from the remembrance of Allah, and from prayer: will ye not then abstain?" (Almaida 91).

Here it is a kind gesture from God to forbid drinking and gambling because it poisons the Character that controls our minds and causes hostility and hatred among us.

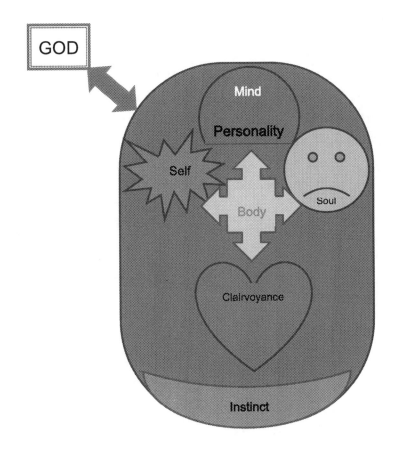

# 5

## SOUL & INSTINCT

As I mentioned earlier that the Human consists of seven elements: the **Mind**, **Self**, **Character**, **Body**, **Spirit** (Soul), **Clairvoyance** (Vision), and the **Instinct** (Commonsense). The spirit is the science of God, who God has given us a small part of it. It has been proven from the Holy Koran that Allah has only breathed into the man from his soul. God said:

"They ask thee concerning the Spirit, Say: "The Spirit by command of my Lord: of knowledge, it is only a little that is communicated to you. If it were Our Will, We could take away that which We have sent thee by inspiration, then wouldst thou find none to plead thy affair in that matter as against Us". (Alisra' 85, 86).

The **Spirit** is from the world of God's command, which does not belong to any time or place, and in the various connotations in the Holy Qur'an suggest to us about **the link with God Almighty, and has nothing to do with the Self** [20]. So neither nor modern science has been able to know what the spirit is. When God almighty created our master Adam from clay and made him a living human being and made his organs work, also on in the fetus, if fetus growth is complete, god has breathed into him from his soul and then he creates his instinct or common sense and the Clairvoyance. God always supports the believers in him with his spirit. Thus the breath of God's spirit may be a support or connection and proximity to God almighty to the man. Also, Qur'an is a spirit inspired by God to his prophet.

**Then Spirit maybe not the life, but connection and proximity to God.**

And God knows better. God said:

"Thou wilt not find any people who believe in Allah and His Messenger, even though....For such, He has written Faith in their hearts, and strengthened them with a Spirit from Himself..." (Almujadala 22).

When the man dies, his **soul** goes out from his body, and also knowledge in his mind fades. But as for the **Self**, it goes back to her God in the Isthmus. The Body wears out and decomposes into hydrocarbons gases: Methane, Ethan and Phosphine...etc., these gases oxidizes or ignites as soon as it comes into contact with air oxygen. If a person drowns in the sea and is eaten by fish, the body turns into a hydrocarbon food for fish. And God knows better.

Some ask: If we read a message, then words and names enter our mind, what goes in our minds? Ink or paper, and where does their meaning settle? Is it our brain, or in our heart, or where? Here as Dr. Muhammad

Shahrour [21] stated that Allah almighty has all the words and knowledge of everything, and what is given to us (believer or nonbeliever) as a Spirit is a very little part of knowledge. The more a human comes up with scientific research, the more his spirit increase its knowledge, but he will not reach the perfection of the knowledge sought by his Creator, who knows everything, no matter how much he discovers, no matter how he invents, develops and researches science, engineering, medicine and literature or all sciences. By God willing, He will erase all the knowledge that has been revealed to us.

God has given something of his spirit to man only and has not given it to other creatures, because man is a creature with Clairvoyance and awareness other than animals. Therefore, maybe when the man dies, his Soul may fade away and science fades from his brain, but God knows better.

God taught Adam all the names. God taught us and teaches us from some of his knowledge. God taught us the languages and names of things. God taught us chemistry, physics, arithmetic, and many others. He is God who knows everything. As for the animal, it has no Spirit; otherwise, a donkey can make a car. But God gave all creatures Self and **Instinct** to multiply and grow, as well as to humans, but God knows the Spirit better.

In my opinion, as I mentioned earlier, God gave man the **Clairvoyance** (vision), without the rest of other

21

creatures. Clairvoyance is the power of perception and acumen. It is science, lessons, and experience of thinking that is not imitation, which is not found in animals, for example. With his vision, the human can watch, think, work, develop, express, and argue in his opinion in clear or developmental language other than an animal. Therefore man was able to develop his life and adapt nature to serve him, while the animal remains as created thousands of years ago as it is.

For the **Clairvoyance**, perhaps its location is the heart of man, God said:

"Do they not travel through the land, so that their hearts may thus learn wisdom and their ears may thus learn to hear? Truly it is not their eyes that are blind, but their hearts which are in their breasts" (Hajj 46).

God said: "Nay, man will be evidence against himself" (Alqyama 14)

As for the Self, it is not from the physical world, it may be a kind of energy from the hereafter world, and for which science is now baffled to know, but it has a weight according to one of the experiments [33]; on a man who lost his weight immediately after his death 22 grams. It was reported that some of those who died during surgeries, then returned to life, were witnesses of what they do with him. Also, laws of material life do not apply to the Self; when sleep, we do not feel the time. God said:

"It is Allah that takes the self at death, and those that did not die during their sleep those on whom He

has passed the decree of death, He keeps back..."
(Alzumar 42)

".... And their selves may perish in their very denial
of Allah" (Altaobah 55).

Perish means getting out from the body, the one
that exceeds to another world is the Self, but the Soul
fades, or it returns to its divine source.

God said:

"O that Self, in complete rest and satisfaction,
Come back thou to thy Lord, well pleased, and well-
pleasing into Him" (Alfajr 27, 28)

God said also:

"I do call to witness the Resurrection Day, And I do
call to witness the self-reproaching Self" (Alqyamah 1,2)

God said, as words of our master Joseph:

"Nor do I absolve my Self of blame, the Self is
certainly prone to evil...". (Yosef 53)

God has created the Self of human beings before
the pot of the body, God said:

"It is We who created you, then gave you shape,
then We bade the angels prostrate to Adam, and they
prostrate, not so Iblis, He refused to be of those who
prostrate" (Alaa'raf 11).

There are levels of self-esteem, know the Self
inside you:

(a) **Reassuring Self:** It is the satisfied soul, it is the
higher degree a reproach Self, it has gone beyond
the stage of blame, beliefs in the hereafter and

the day of the Qiama, it is merciful, it is not afraid of death or the torment of the hereafter, because within her it has satisfied her Creator, and it hopes for his mercy and love for her, it sees in the Holy Quran guidance and thinks about his miracles and in the grace of God on her.

(b) **Allaoama Self:** (Reproach Self), it is failing to obey God, it blames herself, it believes in the hereafter and on the Day of Resurrection, it loves life and maybe merciful, but it is afraid of death and the torment of the grave and burning her skin with fire, because it always fears God and torments on the Day of Resurrection, and hopes for his mercy.

(c) **Heretic Self:** That is, the one who disbelieved in the hereafter and the day of judgment, and says this world and then nothing, it lives anyway, not interested (sabehlala), i.e. an indifferent sin, or empty without principles, may be merciful, but it is afraid to die because it loses the life it loves, with a twig at every joy.

The human brain is a living substance as long as the Self in it. Other creatures also have brains but with Self, not Spirit. Animals are nations like us but we do not feel it. And God knows better.

**In a certain area of a creature's brain or body, there is an analytical site it is the Instinct or common sense.** A Character or Conscience from which good or evil traits are produced, found in the creature. It is the kind of nature and the type of behavior that depends on the biological genetic instinct of the creature. This analytical site is located somewhere in the bodies of all creatures, whether it is an animal, a plant, or atoms of materials. It is the reason for the analytical behavior or specific automatic intelligence of all creatures. Spirit has nothing to do with that. For example; the crow, the dog, and the lion all have a percentage of analytical intelligence. As well as the plant adapts to the direction of light and the environment and some of them hunt insects intelligently.

For example, birds and some fish and animals migrate thousands of miles and return to their place, because God has created a sense of place and a sense of direction with their instincts. While there is no such instinct in man, if a human is lost in a forest, he cannot guide without a compass.

The ratio and type of this instinct or this spontaneous intelligence vary from creature to creature... Of course, the human being has special and the highest percentage, because the human body demands a lot. The Human was created on the earth to build it; he should be god's successor on the earth. Animals and plants are instinctively intelligent only to keep the species and sex. We also observe the instinctive intelligence in bacteria, fungi, viruses, and even material crystals. The crystallization of the table salt cube, the crystallization of sugar the shape of monocline, and the crystallization of silicon is hexagonal. So where ever these materials are, in America or Asia, Besides, each of these crystals has specific instinctive qualities that interact with light, magnets, and with electricity with specific intelligence.

All creatures act and behave according to their instincts or common sense created by God in their composition because they were afraid to be free-will, except the human, he asked his Lord to be free-will, he is unjustly ignorant, he wanted to have his will instinctively free to do what he likes. God said:

"We did indeed offer the Trust to the Heavens and the Earth and the mountains; but they refused to undertake it; being afraid thereof: but man undertook it, he was indeed unjust and foolish" (Alahzab 72).

We carried the will as we were chromosomes (RNA) in the back of our father Adam before we were in this world.

In a more general sense, we can say that **Instinct is the creation of a healthy fitness for the creature to deal with the environment (Common Sense),** it is a cognitive sense of the creature to deal with the environment and the circumstances in which it lives. God placed it in his creature at the birth of his whole so that it is consistent with the method of the creature created by God on him. Our Prophet Mohammad said:

"Every child is born on Fitrah (instinct), also the beast produces a whole beast, and do you feel it is out of shape?"

# 6

## KNOWLEDGE SEEKING IS AN OBLIGATION

Seeking science, knowledge, and the meditation on everything in this universe is a duty from God to every human being. God has honored man over all creatures by blowing him out of his soul, creating clairvoyance in humans, and making him sane and his successor on the earth.

**Science and work are the foundation of civilization, progress, happiness, and strength of nations.** For this, many verses and hadiths came to honor science, scholars, and workers:

God said:

"...Those truly fear Allah, among His Servants, who know: for Allah is exalted in Might, Oft-Forgiving" (Fater 28)

God said:

"There is no god but He: that is the witness of Allah, His angels, and those endued with knowledge, standing firm on justice...." (Al Emran 18)

God said:

"... Say; "Are those equal, those who know and those who do not know? It is those who are endued with understanding that receives admonition" (Alzumar 9)

God said:

"And say: work, soon will Allah observe your work, and His messenger, and the believers..." (Altaubah 105).

Our Prophet Muhammad (pbuh) said:

"The scholar is preferred over worshiper as my virtue over your lowest."

He also said:

"Knowledge seeking is obligatory for every Muslim."

So what is Knowledge and which type of science?

Science does not come from the man himself, but it is from God who gives it to a man if he seeks it, whether he is a believer or not. The Creator has placed in his creation for man the attribute of vision (the Clairvoyance), thought, meditation, and learning. Science has its origins from time immemorial. Knowledge has accumulated and continues to accumulate. It is sperm from the spirit of God, the Knowledgeable of everything. The whole Qur'an is a concentrated science. What we are aware of every day of scientific discoveries; such as the earth's gravity and magnetism, the rotation of the earth and the stars in their Orbits, the expansion of the universe, the shrinking of the land area on Earth, and many others in physics, chemistry, and medicine and so on since God created the Earth and beyond. These are only details of the verses of the Holy Qur'an which is in our hands. In other words, if we think about many verses of the Qur'an in-depth and scientifically, it will lead us to understand many sciences, i.e. whenever we are aware, recognize and sought by science and work; many truths will emerge and appear to us for this universe.

Knowledge, as I heard its definition from Sheikh Mitwali al-Sharawi [25], may God have mercy on him, has two folds:

1 -  Knowledge of religion and its origins.
2 -  Science of the universe and its branches of inanimate (sun, moon, physics, and...), plant (fixed living), animal (moving living), human (medicine, etc.) and work.

The cosmologists are practically in their hands millions of signs and miracles. If they succeeded and they were intelligent and bright-minded, they were inspired to believe in God. There are many in this world, who found the miracles of the Holy Quran. Scientific facts in their hands and became a believer in God. In our time, the French scientist Maurice Bocai (30) and many others from Thailand, America, Japan, Canada, Germany, and Spain are other scholars of the past, such as Newton who believed in a monotheistic God (34), Quilliam and Stanley of Britain (45), and many others who have been Muslim or have acknowledged the greatness of the message of Our Lord Muhammad.

Opinion Newsweek

**Can the Power of Prayer Alone Stop a Pandemic like the Coronavirus? Even the Prophet Muhammad Thought Otherwise | Opinion**

CRAIG CONSIDINE

On 3/17/20 at 1:06 PM

Muhammad, the prophet of Islam, over 1,300 years ago.

While he is by no means a "traditional" expert on matters of deadly diseases, Muhammad nonetheless had sound advice to prevent and combat a development like COVID-19.

Muhammad said: "If you hear of an outbreak of plague in a land, do not enter it; but if the plague outbreaks out in a place while you are in it, do not leave that place."

He also said: "Those with contagious diseases should be kept away from those who are healthy."

Muhammad also strongly encouraged human beings to adhere to hygienic practices that would keep people safe from infection. Consider the following hadiths, or sayings of Prophet Muhammad

# 7

## KNOWLEDGE, FAITH & BELIEF

**Faith and belief are the certification from heart, with the truth of something or accepting the truth of something that does not fall under the human senses, i.e. perhaps rejected by your conscious mind and your five senses.** Such as believing in God and paradise, fire, believing in the greatness of this country, or believing in yourself that you can do something..... Faith here is a way of thinking, or it is a position of the mind, or it is an internal certainty, which is to know that what you are thinking is perfectly acceptable in your conscious mind and will be embodied in your unconscious mind and will be clear.

Faith performs miracles, whether it's true or a myth.

Faith and believing in something without knowledge, reason, or guidance, whether it be a behavioral, social, or religious belief without justification, proofs, or thoughtful constants, are forces that can sometimes destroy our lives and will be an obstacle to our happiness, or be a reason to make us happy.

God said:

"...They say: nay! We shall follow the ways of our fathers. What even though their fathers were void of wisdom and guidance." (Albaqara 170).

Why do we have to take and recognize certain things as long as they are unproven and untested and have been received as habits and societal behavior for hundreds of years? It is necessary for an intelligent human being to re-examine them and test them based on new existing data, the development of our knowledge, and the development of our minds and ideas. To know what benefits us and what harms us in the reality of our affairs and its compatibility with the constants of faith in our religion.

Al Qur'an is science and guidance, the words Science and Knowledgeable have been mentioned in many verses. God distinguishes those who are Knowledgeable from those who are not Knowledgeable and believe in things according to customs and traditions without using thought.

Not only knowledge of the constants of religion, but rather in nature, morals, and that entire God has created in this world. Science is the foundation of civilizations and the progress and power of man. Because of this many verses and hadiths came to honor science and scientists. God said:

"...Say: Are those equal, those who know and those who do not know? It is those who are endued with understanding that receives admonition" (Alzumar 9)

"There is no God but He: That is the witness of Allah, His angels, and those endued with knowledge..." (Al Imran 18)

"...Those truly fear Allah, among His servants, who know: for Allah is exalted in Might, Oft-Forgiving" (Fater 28).

It has been said that: "science is light, and ignorance is darkness",

It was also said: "Ignorance is revenge and science is mercy."

Therefore, seeking knowledge in Islam laws is considered obligatory, not intended only the knowledge of nature, religion, and medicine, but also the knowledge of all what we do in our lives and behavior, and to know the validity and compatibility with the approach to God's.

The Messenger of Allah (PBUH) said:

"The Scholars preferred to the worship, as my preference to your lowers".

What is science? As Sheikh Al-Sha'rawi explained: Science has two folds:

1) Knowledge of religion and its Assets.
2) Knowledge of the universe and its branches of Inanimate - (physics and chemistry), plant (fixed organisms), animal (moving), human

(medicine), add to that psychology, economics, and business.

The cosmologists have millions of signs and miracles in their hands. They will be guided to believe in God and his apostles, If they succeeded and open-minded.

Simply "Knowledge gives us pleasure", Even if I made myself a cup of coffee, I'm going to have it with pleasure, because I know what's in it and how I made it.

Ali bin abu-talib said: "Win knowledge, you live forever. Then people dead, but that of knowledge is alive."

# 8

## SLUGGISH DOCTRINE

When I was young studying in Vienna / Austria, at the time, I was not managing the Qur'an. I floated looking for a principle or a religion that I understand. I found a group of people who convert to Mormon doctrine, with some of their information makes sense, but some things need to be clarified. The priest told me after I rained him with questions and inquiries about mysterious things in their faith, such as the means of divine commands from time to time, he said: firstly: believe in our faith without long thinking, then you will understand and believe in it. I was not convinced and did not believe in their faith.

- While in the Islamic religion, God commands us in many places, to use our minds and then believe:
- "Maybe they're **wise**", mentioned in Quran 22 times.
- "They could **see**", mentioned 13 times.
- "Those who **give thought**", mentioned 11 times.

"Seek to **understand** the Qur'an", mentioned twice.

However, the divine commands and prohibitions in the holy Qur'an are from the creator to a creature, they are not equal, God commands should be applied without controversy, and their advantages may be known after application, but we can manage their thoughts in our minds.

Dr. Sergei Savilev (Russian researcher, head of the Nervous System development Laboratory of the Russian Academy of Sciences) in brain neurology [22,23], tells us that when we think we consume more than 25% of the body's energy in the Brain's thinking because the nerves of the Brain become working with its full capacity. Whereas, the consumption of energy for thinking becomes less than 8% if we accept things without carefully thinking about them, thus the nerves of our brain decay, some secretes which are chemical substances, are produced that numb the brain, and the human becomes inert, that is to say, the inactivity of the mind of man will be idiot, i.e. those who are sluggish (rabble).

People are of three types:

1) The **Scientist**: is the one who is proficient in his research.
2) The **Learner:** (intellectual) is the one who researches and receives information and experiences from different sources so that he can understand life.

Both, the Scientist and the Learner develop their cognitive abilities to think.

3) And the third category is the **Sluggish**, those are who do not try to understand, and to view what is going on around them, but they accept what is said to them without thinking well, and they are many. Sluggish people are easy to drive like a flock of sheep. They don't use their mind to understand what is going on around them, or what is said. It will be easier for them to accept what other people around them said, they say: "as long as everyone says this, then it's true". This last category concentrates in their minds rust, i.e. iron rust, if long time not used and exposed to moisture then its use is void. Rust in mind is the effects of cognitive poverty and reading desertification, which is the interaction of the mind with mental stagnation. By stop thinking will make the mind comfortable, and in the colloquial language, we say that this person has a rusted mind.

Modern philosophy defines thinking [24] as **"a structured and purposeful cognitive process that we use to understand the world around us to devise decisions"**. Thinking or foresight, which is a fundamental characteristic that God has given to the human mind, it develops with us so that we can use it to solve the problems that face us in this world, and we can develop our ability to think in systematic and orderly ways:

1) Focus our attention on everything that goes around us; examine our thoughts and other people's ideas on topics of interest to us.
2) Create an intellectual sense in us by practicing thinking and how others look at a particular topic, and with a lot of reading and viewing.

Psychology distinguishes types of thinking, including:

(A) **Traditional Thinking** or Superstitious Thinking: People use it as a blind imitation to relax their brain, it is simple, naïve does not depend on scientific or logical reasons, and this includes a high percentage of the society, or what they are described as the sluggish thinkers.

(B) **Critical thinking** or scientific thinking, and here the individual relies on personal assumptions and the opinions of others to challenge assumptions and determine their importance, and to reach a conclusion by rational judgment, and this includes many scientists, intellectuals, and learners. This thinking increases the energy consumption of the brain, expands it, and creates a mature, creative, and thought-thinking human being. This is the thinking that our God always asks of us, for faith without reflection and foresight in what we see from the creatures and miracles that God reminds us of the Holy Qur'an, what they are, and why they are like this, how they existed and why. This type of thinking lets us prove our faith and be sure of the existence of God, the Creator of everything.

(C) **Creative thinking** or philosophical thinking, it is a process that promotes the development of new and unique ideas for solutions to problems, or inventions. This includes inventors who dare to modernize societies, and they are few.

I hope from my God that we have always thought of "Critical" and think about our religion and all things in our lives.

# 9

## THE DESTINY

I heard who says: If God has determined my destiny, why would he make me accountable for what I do? And if everything that is going on in this world is God willing, what is the sin of human beings?

Answer: Yes with the difference: what a man does is **by his own will**, and fate has nothing to do with it. The fact that God knows what we are going to do and what will happen does not mean that he imposed it on us.

For the creature to be free-willed in this worldly life is trust before God, all God's creatures have been sorry or afraid to be a center of trust for God so that they may be free to carry this trust except man, and he wishes to have freedom of thought. Therefore, the freedom of thought was given only to man and placed in the formation of our chromosomes in the creation of our grandfather Adam. God made the conscience and intention of man his own, which is forbidden for others. The rest of the other creatures were created by God with his instinct or a marching instinct.

God says:

"Every self will be held in pledge for its deeds" (Almuddather 38)

And He says:

"We did indeed offer the Trust to the Heavens and the Earth and the Mountains; but they refused to undertake it, being afraid thereof: but man undertook it,-He was indeed unjust and foolish" (Alahzab 72).

The philosopher Freud [15] said that instinct is raw, and the will of man is controlled by it.

One of the pillars of Islam is to believe in god's destiny, good and evil.

So, is man free to choose his way or obligated?

"God judges and He predestines". To understand this statement, we have to understand the composition of humans. Here I quote from the ideas of the Sheikh Mohammed Mutually Al-Sahrawi [16];

God has destined for man in two regions, these control his destiny:

1 - **The first region:** In all that <u>falls into man's</u> **<u>internal organs</u>** <u>or falls on him</u> **from outside** <u>without his will</u>, here **human has <u>no choice</u> and has no power in that**. God judge and God predestine. "God simplifies the livelihood for those who want and appreciate". God set laws and rules in this world, which I mentioned earlier. If human accepts and adheres to it, he will be pleased and happy in his life, and God

41

will make his life easy whatever it was. But if a man breaks the laws; his life will be miserable and naughty, even if he got the money and prestige he wished.

God said: "But whosoever turns away from My Message, verily for him is a life narrowed down, and We shall raise him blind on the Day of Judgment". (Taa-Haa 134)

2 -  **The second region:** is suitable for his vision (Clairvoyance) and the human being is free. It is the act that falls **from the human being from his will and choice**, and the human being here is in charge of what he does, in what happens in his Self - without the physical existence that God has granted- and is unique to the freedom of will. There is nothing that prevents what in a man atrophied in him and what he does. Your thoughts produce your beliefs and this will produce your words, these are followed by your actions that define your habits, and your habits describe your behavior and character that lead you to your destiny for good or evil.

But, when we establish in ourselves the controls of desires, that God has placed for us in our religion and our good nature. We have implied that God will give us happiness and become masters of ourselves, not slaves to our desires, god willing... God said:

"So he who gives in charity and fears Allah, and testifies to the best, We will indeed make smooth for him the path to Bliss. But he who is a greedy miser and thinks himself sufficient, and gives the lie to the best, We will indeed make smooth for him the path to Misery" (Allyl 10).

This means that **God has always left us the freedom of initiative and action with our intention**, and then god's will comes with his justice, and he will **increase us with guidance or misdirection according to our intention** (And we guided him to help either, thankful or disbelieving). This means that **God's destiny is of the kind of intention of the self,** (and what you want is only god's will.) That means destiny will come from God.

As long as God granted us part of the freedom as we wanted, thus he imposed on us a great responsibility. It is a freedom that is responsible for what we do. Of course, responsibility is followed by evaluation and accountability.

**In conclusion, human freedom is real, despite the limits and resistances that can exist around it.**

As what we think is a success, with a lot of money and notability, it is actually for evaluation and an examination from God in this world. Such is the same poverty and poverty is also an assessment and an examination, God says:

"Now, as for the man, when his Lord trieth him, giving him honor and gifts, then saith he: My Lord hath honored me", But when He trieth him restricting his subsistence for him, then saith he: "My Lord hath humiliated me", Nay…" (Alfajr 15-17).

The injustice of others, jealousy, envy, gambling, and malice abuse are degrees of suicide, wasting life, and freedom. Then God will bless us with unhappiness. For example:

- A worker neglects the work assigned to him… Result: He's out of his job.
- A trader cheats in his wares… Result: his wares are down.
- A man whose words are lies… The result: He will be known by God and to those who know him as a liar; he loses people's trust in him and loses their respect for him.
- An unjust manager…The result: no sincerity in the work of his employees.
- I want to burn a house; I'm the one who gives the house a match stick… The fire begins to work, it is a chemical law created by God between material and oxygen, but I am the one who decided to burn the house, it is not God's will.

If you thank God for what you are, to be merciful to God's creatures, to seek good for all, to leave backbiting, gossip and cunning, and what angers God, all to seek God's pleasure. This will bring you goodness, comfort, reassurance, and more to be happy in all the circumstances of your life because God loved you and took care of you.

# 10

## THE DEVINE BOOK

The holy Qur'an is the word of God Almighty. It is not a creature as claimed by the Mu'tazila during the days of the Caliph al-Ma'mun, because God's creatures have a lifetime and end. I look at Qur'an as a miracle painting, every word and letter in its position has a special meaning, the Qur'an in it thousands or millions of images that God created in his book, it portrays of science, morals, and exhortations, and advice to the worlds from the past, to the present and future, no one can interpret them except God, but in each era, we can meditate and cognate the reflection of each verse meaning for that era, God said:

"…but no one knows its hidden meaning except Allah. And those who are firmly grounded in knowledge say: We believe in the book…" (Al-Emran 7).

Therefore, the noble Qur'an is an eternal book for every time and place, so I believe that it is difficult to understand its thoughts at the time being for all eras **except for the firm and constants in the Shari'ah** such as Islamic laws, acts of worship, inheritance, the

position of religion towards women and orphans, etc…
But we can understand the reflection of the meaning of
the verses, so the honorable interpreters –with God's
help - have worked hard and given us some ambiguous
or unclear meanings of some verses for their era, and
perhaps it is difficult to be convinced of it today. The
Almighty said:

"For every massage is a limit of time, and soon shall
ye know it" (Alana'am 67)

"And ye shall certainly know the truth of it after a
while" (S~ad 88)

"And say: "Praise be to Allah, Who will soon show
you His Signs…" (Alnaml 93).

Nobody can interpret the Qur'an in the literal
sense even if he possesses the talent for huge
information in the Arabic language, hadith, natural
science, psychology, sociology, life sciences, peoples'
life sciences, and etc… but we can perceive some
thoughts and opinions, then we say we believe in God.
Because the Qur'an is a book of religion and it is a
way of life, not a book of philosophy, it suffices with
flashing, ablution, and hint, symbol and sign in most of
its verses, and stories.

When I meditate Qur'an and looking at the
interpretation of some interpreters, some pleasant
thoughts come to my mind:

Is the method and terminology of the Hereafter
understandable as it is in this world??? Of course not,

because in the Hereafter there is Horon Een (mere eye ladies), and rivers of milk and honey....!! What if someone cannot tolerate honey! Is there an account of time in the Hereafter? Are we growing old? Will we be hungry???

For example, each dynamic system has a different time than any other dynamic system! That's why the time in our life is different from that of the hereafter! In other words, when we enter into a dream while we sleep, our time is not the same in the period of vigilance. In a dream, we may be exposed to events and information for years, but the sleep time is probably less than half an hour.

Since God created humans, He sent down divine books and the Qur'an guiding for a decent way of living, in this world of testing only. But after JudgDay, troublingly, this approach does not apply in the afterlife! Before our master Muhammad, peace and blessings are upon him, **God was sending a messenger to every nation with instructions and a simplified approach that suits their cognitive ability and their living conditions**, and the message of our master Muhammad, peace be upon him, was the conclusion for every time and place.

Therefore, **the understanding of the thoughts of a Qur'an verse is according to the scientific and cultural level of those who wanted to understand its significance, and their understanding guides**

**them to the thoughts that their life will be happier. The people of the past tense were guided to some thoughts and understood according to their cultural and scientific level...** As for the people of the present, we have deconstructed some meanings and thoughts of verses. And our grandchildren and grand-grandchildren will discover other thoughts and connotations that help them understand for a better life.

Perhaps someone who says that the Holy Qur'an is all talk about fire, torment, and woe ... Yes, there is a lot of warning to those who do not understand or think, while it contains more of great meanings, wisdom, sermons, and morals, and it contains scientific miracles for those who understand and reason, Almighty said:

"...But none reject our signs except only a perfidious wretch" (Luqman 32)

The number of verses of the Noble Qur'an[4] is 6236 verses, of which the verses of legislation are 535 verses, but in the Great Qur'an about 1395 verses speak of science, knowledge, vision, and remembrance of the miracles that God created in and around us. As for most of the rest, they are real stories of peoples who have passed through, a judgment for a sermon, and another to contemplate the judgment of God.

God set instinct for man in the formation chromosomes since the time of our master Adam, and from him, this code was passed on to all the nations in this world from the descendants of Adam, peace upon him. Every characteristic of this instinct has a cause and purpose. So, to eat an apple, we have to plant an apple tree, and eating an apple is necessary for our growth. Likewise, to multiply, we must find a partner, and sex is an instinct or instinct to multiply, and so on.

But God also set in his Qur'an regulations and laws to fine-tune every aspect of instinct ... for example, God Almighty said regarding the subject of anger:

"...Repel with what is better: then will he between whom and thee was hatred become as it were thy friend and intimate" (Fuselat 34).

As for the world of the hereafter, it is another deferent world. The reasons do not need a cause, you will live forever, do not grow gray, and do not need to grow or multiply, if you want an apple that makes you feel in your mouth. Many things are difficult to recognize now in our minds... only God knows it.

**Then, laws of the Hereafter are not the same as the laws of the existing world**. In the Holy Qur'an, our Lord has set for us a Simulation of what we will be in Heaven and Hell so that humans can understand and accommodate the situation in the hereafter. Rivers of milk and honey, the rubies, corals, and the Horen Een (mere eye ladies) will not be as in our world. Also, the fire of the hereafter maybe not the fire of this world... It's a simulation to make it easier for us to understand the meaning. Here humans need the power of faith in God and his book and the hereafter without having the ability to go into understanding the details!! And God knows better, God said:

"With him are the keys of unseen, the treasures that none knoweth but He…" (Alan'am 59).

But as long as we believe that the Noble Qur'an is from God, we have to believe in the occults that God has told us:

"Who believe in the unseen, are steadfast in prayer… they are on true guidance and it is these who will prosper" (Al Bakara 5-3)

# 11

## LAWS OF LIFE

Why does a person become rich and another poor, why does someone succeed in reaching what he wants and another fails, why is that man happy and I am unfortunate??

We live in a universe that the Creator created it with laws and balance in everything; these are signs for people who contemplate. To answer the previous questions, we must understand the laws of life, in particular, the laws of energy in human Self:

The laws of arithmetic: 2 times 3 equals 6, the laws of physics: light goes in a straight line, the laws of chemical reactions ($2H_{2\ g}^+ + O_g^- = H_2O_{l)}$, etc. ...

Laws of the universe: the sun and the moon each swim in its Orbit and the sun runs for its stable.

The laws of morality: smile in my face, and then I will smile in your face. Lie to me, then I will lose confidence in you and I will not believe your words later. Damn me evil, that will happen to you sooner or later.

All these laws are absolute and unbiased to race, color, or religion that does not differentiate between a believer and an infidel. Almighty said:

"It is Allah Who has sent down the Book in Truth and the Balance..." (Ashora 17)

"And the Firmament has He raised high, and He has set up the Balance" (Alrahman 7).

"We sent afore time our messengers with clear signs and sent down with them the Book and the Balance..." (Alhadeed 25)

"And the earth We have spread out, set thereon mountains firm and immovable, and produced therein all kinds of things in due Balance" (Alhijr 19).

The Creator also tells us that he created all pairs in a balance between a male and a female:

"Glory to Allah, Who created in pairs all things that the earth produces, as well as their kind and things of which they do not know" (Yaseen 36).

The Self also has the absolute law of gravity between one person and another, the <u>law of attraction</u>[7] - as it is called - not only between one body and the Earth but also with all bodies on the surface of the Earth, because objects have energy and because attraction comes from the energy present in bodies. The attraction strength is directly proportional to the product of the mass of the two objects divided by the square of the distance between them. The Moon revolves around the Earth, the Earth revolves around the Sun, but the centrifugal force will keep the moon away from the Earth, and the Earth away from the Sun, the more the center of attraction loses something of its energy, i.e. after thousands of years one earth day maybe 25 hours and one Sun year maybe 13 months, these are the laws of God the Creator.

Likewise, the laws of energy, even the energy in motion, sound, light, and rays. Energy consists of frequency waves or vibrations that have a distinct length, width, and speed, such as the energy emitted by the mobile phone that we carry.

**I believe that the Self is a type of energy; changing its frequency, its attraction or broadcast differs;** and each Self has special waves. But God knows best. **The point of reception and transmission in a person to the frequencies of ideas is the subconscious mind as defined by psychologists**[13]. As we use our thinking, we consume energy from our bodies and transmit it in certain forms, this image will be printed in our subconscious and begins to transmit certain frequencies, the image can be a liked image or an evil image, and whenever we change the image in ourselves the frequencies will change.

The Prophet (pbuh) said: "Be optimistic, you find the good".

Have you ever noticed that what you need may happen to you?

Or maybe someone came in front of you, whom you were thinking about him?

Or maybe you found your life partner, where you will be surprised that he had one way or another connected to your life without your prior knowledge?

Or did you go to the right place at the wrong time?

All these are proof that the law of attraction works in your life. Here we can define the law of attraction for man as **the law that has in your life attracted ideas that dominate your mind positively or negatively**[36, 37].

The pictures in our imagination could be the money we dream about, the way we collect them, the certificate we aspire to, or the misery we are in, etc...

From the aforementioned, I affirm that there is **nothing in life called luck or coincidence**. Everything that takes place around us has laws established by the Creator of this life, so everything that happens in existence or ourselves is subject to the frequencies emitted by our minds, good or bad. So to be happy we have to hold our thoughts accountable to ourselves and others. Is it good or bad?

The personality of a human is within himself, it is the values, and the principles he sets for himself, it is the concepts that are difficult to change. Personality determines our apparent behavior, which is our actions; we can change our actions according to the situation. Many philosophers discuss the relationship between human thoughts and actions, and between a person's personality and behavior. **Our thoughts define our personality, which becomes words and words that turn into actions that in turn constitute habits and behavior, which in turn determines the destiny of a person** by interacting with the universe around him in various pleasant and difficult circumstances, meaning **no luck or coincidences**:

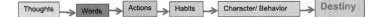

Science has not yet been able to obtain many details about the secrets and types of transmitters and receivers for the physical and psychological forces of attraction and expulsion, but we have to understand how to use it to our advantage, an intelligent person can use it to his advantage.

For example, the law of gravity was a reason in the flow of water from top to bottom, so the human being used the Potential Energy stored in the upper water to produce electric energy to make better life ... while a naughty man, an inconsiderate man throws himself from the top of a building, empties the potential energy stored in his body, and dies!!

Likewise, your smile in the face of your brother bounces back a smile from your brother in your face, and your disdain for your brother will return to you his disdain for you, love of goodness for others brings you all goodness!! ... These are laws!

Now, what kind of thoughts is in our subconscious and conscious mind? If we continue to think positively to dream and assure ourselves that we will be rich, and do not worry about that, but to work hard on it, by all means, we will, after years, become rich. But when wealth becomes the property of our hands, then we are haunted and worried by thoughts of losing our money, and whether we will be back poor, perhaps we will lose money or sure we will live a miserable life.

That is why our thoughts must always be positive. We should believe and praise God Almighty and do not fear poverty. Always expect what you want and do not expect what you do not want. Always say thank God for what He gave you. God said:

"And remember! Your Lord caused to be declared: If ye are grateful, I will add more (favors) unto you, But if ye show ingratitude, truly My punishment is terrible indeed" (Ibrahim 7).

When I was 50 years old, I got Rheumatoid Arthritis, and I started walking with crutches, climbing stairs hard, and I can't carry even a thin taboo between my fingers, I interred the hospital and became a prisoner of the treatments. I was told that this disease will reach the lungs and heart and be the end. I said to my wife: "my dream was to float the world with you when I retire, but it seems that the estimate is not". Months passed, I convinced myself: "I will be stronger than this disease. I insisted, despite the pain; to walk standing without help, eat my food and drink myself, then will practice the desired sports, and will live happily". I was sure of this because I trusted my God then trust myself, and was not afraid of any result. Later, when the disease disappeared, I'm moving around the world.

Any incurable disease can be treated from within oneself, and follow the right nutrition, diet, or gymnastic with appropriate medication. Man is the product of his thoughts [8].

# 12

# POWER OF SUBCONSCIOUS MIND

The human brain works in two lines:

1) **The conscious mind**: the mind that controls logical thinking, chooses and decides willingly what suits him, decides what he wants, and determines what he believes in and what his beliefs are. He is the director and guides for all the processes of the world through the five senses. It only works when the human being is awake.

2) **The inner or subconscious mind**: accepts everything that is given to it or believes in it without thinking or analysis, because it is like the soil of the earth, which the conscious mind cultivates in it. The subconscious works 24 hours, it also supervises the work of the body's vital organs such as heart, breathing, digestion, etc.....

I read the book "The Power of your subconscious Mind" by the scientist Joseph Murphy[13], which talks about the power of our subconscious mind (unconscious mind), and delves into the details of the influence of the subconscious mind on human life, how a man can use it: makes it obedient to him to achieve what he wishes. Murphy presented in his book a tremendous amount of practical experiences, as well as talking about various ways and methods that the human mind can convince his subconscious to achieve a desire. In his book, he gives a realistic example that he says it was tried. But I'm not entirely convinced of the psychological justifications he's given. But when I discussed it with my wife, she reminded me of the Qur'an verse in which our God said in Surat al-Thunder:

"For each such person, there are angels in succession, before and behind him: they guard him by command of Allah. Allah does not change a person's lot unless they change what in their selves…." (Alraad 11).

What comes to my mind here is that God ordered angels to guard the human being (believer and unbeliever), these angels are commanded by the human subconscious mind (good or evil), **and the subconscious mind then has supernatural abilities beyond the limits of human with the help of these angels (which are ordered by God to obey the human subconscious)**.

If you atrophied well, you succeed, and if you atrophied evil, you lose. Then God will not change what in you unless you change what in yourself. Faith and desire stem from the conscious mind, and the subconscious mind believes what the conscious mind believes in, and executes its desires with the help of these angels. God knows better.

I don't know how it's done, but I am convinced that it's done, I have personally experienced such cases, some of them consciously and persistently from me, some of them with an internal desire without insistence. If we examine what is going on around us, we realize that there is an effect of that noble Quranic verse and its meaning becomes clear. The problem is how to convince your subconscious mind of something, how is the technology of persuasion!?

Our conscious mind thinks, decides, and feels by our five senses. While our subconscious mind does not recognize place or time [14], it realizes what is around it with the Clairvoyance sense (the ability to gain information about an object through extrasensory perception), when the five senses are not ready, the subconscious mind has a sense of clairvoyance or sensitivity or sharpness in perception so it can leave your body and travel to the far or dive into the feelings of others and imagine them. The information is stored in it as a video or a computer, if it wants to remember, then it choose the analog video for the existing case.

Or to make a reproduction of it and study it to find a suitable solution to what is in it now, a wish or solution for a problem.

The subconscious mind thinks and is convinced of what the conscious mind dictates and confirms. For example, if you want to become something, you have to convince your subconscious mind to do so and assure it over and over again. This relationship is only between the conscious and subconscious mind, it is not between you and someone else, and it is not wise to broadcast it to others. Focus on what you want. **The people who make their reality are not afraid of the future, because they know that their reality will be a similar picture to what they drew with their subconscious.**

To believe in being able to achieve something or anything, while working for it, good or bad, to reach what you believe in. To believe from the depths within you that you will become truly rich and successful, or to recover from a disease that is the magic key for getting what you want. Or to believe that you are unhappy, you will become truly unhappy. This is a real operation, but we don't know how it works. Yes, there is magic in the faith with your subconscious mind.

Hard work alone does not lead you to success, but hard work with faith will lead you to reach your goal. Put what you want to be clear in your conscious mind. Prepare your potential and draw its chart, be serious and patient. Your thoughts will pass on to your subconscious mind, and this attracts what you are interested in. Your thoughts will be transformed into words, which in turn into actions and become habits, behavior that leads you to your destiny.

The infinite intelligence of the subconscious mind leads and directs spiritually, mentally, and materially, Murphy lists many examples:

- A 50-year-old woman who has never thought about getting married in her life, but today she dreams of a man comes to marry her. The urgency of that dream continues from within and occupies her for weeks, then her dream comes true*.
- A person who walked 30 km on his feet tired of his leg muscles and fell to the ground and could not walk. He was told: if you wash your feet with this blessed water, you will be back active and follow your walk. He believed in this and did; so he felt active and went back to walk*.
- Prophet Mohammad the Messenger of God told his companions that they would conquer the Empires of the Persians and the Romans, but they were nomads, so they believed in it and worked for him, and it was achieved.

If the conscious mind believes in something, the subconscious mind will act accordingly.

## How to ask your unconscious mind to do something:

Sit in a quiet, secluded place, close your eyes, relax for some time and follow all your body members (legs, hands, heart,) one by one and ask them to relax until you reach the stage of snooze (half-awake). Be affirming of a beautiful fact that everything you ask can be implemented and that God created you and made you better. Or you are not sick and what you feel is temporary, or you are in excellent good health, or surely your request will be fulfilled, repeated that in a haft voice.

Repeat this position for days or even weeks.

Trust and believe in the reality of any idea or plan and when working on it, it will become a reality.

# 13

## SECRET OF RELIANCE ON GOD

Throughout the ages, the human race has encountered difficulties and problems, but the most difficult of these problems have existed in our age. This is the age of evolution, technology, Nano-technology, and quantum mechanics. Many believe that modern science helps solve human psychological problems, but the reality is the opposite. Science in schools, universities, and modern philosophy has not been able to prevent the spread of lies, fraud, drugs, crime, insecurity, anxiety, and fear.

I read in the newspaper, heartbreaking news: The groom gets angry and suffocates his bride on the night of the wedding. The difference of opinion between couples or between one person and another is normal, but to use one of the beatings, killing, or screaming is inhumane behavior. Animals when they get angry use their hands, legs, and teeth because their Clairvoyance (vision) is non-existent, or because they are under-thinking by instinct. God did not blow them out of his soul but gave them the instinct to grow and multiply and preserve their sex.

Life's problems are endless, and we are required to solve them daily"... What are the reasons? Are physical solutions enough?

- Is alcohol, drugs, or sedatives the solution? Its use makes the problem worse and the winner is a trader or psychiatrist.
- Is money a solution? Rich people and rich countries, not helped by money, but money became a burden on them. There is a lot of luxury, drugs, and false pride, so the human being is corrupted. Physical security became a hoax.
- Maybe Technology and Science? The universities could not prevent fear, anxiety, insecurity, and crime spread. The unscrupulous misuse of technology leads to problems.
- Maybe Intelligence? Unfortunately, some times man used this to exploit, increase vileness in wars, and to conquer man's brother.

All those material solutions, without relying on God and acting according to his right guidance on how to live, did not represent the best solution to the problems of man in this world. Drugs, money, science, intelligence, and philosophy all used the tangible material of the nature of our physical formation and ignored or failed to recognize our spiritual composition, and falsely claimed that nature had formed itself.

- What if we look at the faith in the Creator who guarantees everything He created! Faith in our God is open to all human beings.
- God created the believer, the disobedient, and the infidel and ensuring their livelihood. God loves all his creations Muslim and non-Muslim. He is merciful to them on the steps. Merciful with obedient, hard-working, and even infidel, but he do not cherish him or does not satisfy him with his disbelief.
- Yes, let's deal with beliefs... this enters into our Selves; it refines it, satisfies it, and gives it safety... It becomes a tangible fact.
- God said:
  "It is those who believe and confuse not their beliefs with wrong – that are truly in security, for they are on right guidance." (Alan'am 82)
- God said:
  "Who provides them with food against hunger and with security against fear" (Quraish 4).

**Many recognize that God truly exists. But it is difficult for them to understand how relying on God, because mixing of worldly material affairs in their mind. They are confused!!! ...**

God sent the apostles and messengers with evidence to the people to believe in him and be guided. To believe in something, my mind first has to be sure of it. Then certainty proves the faith. The evidence of our Lord Muhammad was not physical, like other prophets, but it was the great Qur'an, which fascinated us, fascinate us now, and will fascinate us with the miracles of God over time. The Qur'an approach depends on faith in the mind to prove certainty.

Islam is not like other beliefs. The Muslim's faith depends on understanding with his mind and his awareness. Islam asks us to use our brain, if we realize logic, certainty is proven. Certainty is the confidence or conviction of the existence of a great power that created this universe and sent the prophets and the Qur'an to guide people. Certainty is trust in the existence of God; it is an inner feeling in humans.

To prove our certainty about the existence of God, we must learn certainty and its practice, because certainty needs to be learned and practiced, to improve the belief in God and to fully depend on him. God is knowledgeable of everything and manages everything. He manages the judiciary and destiny. He left us to use our mind within the borders He drew for us, and asked us to trust Him.

Prophet Mohammad said: "Learned certainty as you learn the Qur'an until you knew it, I am learning it."

There is a beautiful feeling of relying on God, a feeling that gives reassurance and acceptance of what will be, even if it is not what we wanted it to be. I do not claim that religion is the opium of the peoples because opium stops the mind from working, but the Qur'an demands the use of the mind, and it considers opium and alcohol from evil. I say that faith is a beautiful feeling with logic; it changes the Self and delights it. It is only realized by those who deepen their faith in certainty, and learn the following:

- To believe that God will make you happy... And follow his approach... You'll be happy.
- To believe that God will give you success in your work... And follow his approach... You're going to be successful.
- To believe that God will save you from a miserable or sick situation... And follow his approach... Sure you will be saved.
- To believe that everything you didn't have... It's originally not for you.
- To believe that all that God has given you...It is a mercy to you and what prevented from you is wisdom.

There's no such thing as coincidence, or I've arrived at this position with my effort or my intelligence!

Yes, there is no doubt that personal effort and some intelligence are factors for success, and perhaps to failure!!

But the human being strives, and God put your destiny and appreciates the results.

The product of your effort and intelligence will satisfy you if you abide by the faith in God because God will appreciate what satisfies you. Yes, there are rich infidels, and we think that they are successful, but God is testing them, if you looked inside them, you would see them unsatisfied for one reason or another. Believing in God is the key to success for reassured Self, which is to believe that God is your sponsor, returning to him in your affairs. You accept what you are destined to have and be thankful. The idea of believing in God and his Messenger, and **relying on God**, is the same as ending psychological problems and softening the impact of any human being's physical or material problems.

The life of this world as it is a playhouse; it is also a house of happiness and a test for you from God. So God made in it a rich luxuriant and another satisfied thankful, a poor infidel is dissatisfied and another is satisfied. There is an unhappy naughty and a happy believer. Then God left you the choice of what you want to be, for testing you.

There are many examples around us with stories of people who have inherited and lost a lot of money or have lived unhappily despite the riches. People born poor were enriched by God, or happy despite their poverty. And people who have everything they wish for, but they are miserable and some of them are committed suicide.

God said:

"Verily those who say: Our Lord is Allah, and remain firm; on them shall be no fear, nor shall they grieve" (Alahqaf 13).

"It is those who believe and confuse not their beliefs with wrong – that are truly in security, for they are on right guidance" (Alana'am 82).

# 14

# PHILOSOPHY & RELIGION

Philosophy is a tool of science, knowledge, and thought activity, but Islam is the religion of life that does not need philosophy because it is clear.

The human being practiced the philosophy of life or the jurisprudence of life from ancient times in search of the truth and facts of life and its creator, so philosophy was said to be the daughter of religions and the mother of science. In Philosophy man usually seeks the roots of real knowledge and facts, to be convinced or persuades. And knowledge of realism is a true and justified belief by work. Then the facts are valued by work, the facts to our brains are like food for the body, some of which are more delicious to our cognitive sensitivity, and knowledge gives you pleasure, so man always seeks the truth.

The Greek philosopher Aristotle believed that there must be a first reason that created everything, and he created existence and time. But Plato likened the Creator to be an example of ultimate goodness, and there are two worlds: our unperfected real-world, which we live in, and another perfect world with replicas of our world. The philosophers have continued to search for existence until now, and the reason is that man, under his longing to know the Creator, always seeks him with his philosophy. Although God has sent every nation from eternity messengers dedicated to God.

Some believe that without philosophy we do not know the Creator [2], but I am sure that by contemplating the great Qur'an we will be convinced of the existence of the Creator. Because the Qur'an does not need a philosophy, it is all knowledge, intellectual activity, clear facts, and action. They tell us scientific facts and realistic images, showing us the roots of knowledge. Those who think and understand the Qur'an are convinced whether they are scientists, scholars, or living on the street.

Islam is distinguished from philosophy as it is the religion of real life, in the message of Islam, which descended on Our Lord Muhammad a realistic jurisprudence and deeper sciences than philosophy, encompassing all the realities of life in the world and the hereafter, its laws respected all of God creation and transcending the limits of the human mind. And it surpassed its predecessors in the religions and philosophies of the peoples of Greece, India, and China. This is the secret of the speed of its spread at the beginning of the call. However, this spread has encountered and continues to face difficulties,

**because some of those who claim to understand religion, have taken the expiation of the Muslim who researches in the jurisprudence of reality for the Quranic verses,** such as anatomy in medicine, banking transactions, and the definition of Interest (Riba), so that those considered to be taboo. So some of the young people refrained from believing in religion and faith in God????

I do not deny that many of our Muslim ancestors in many villages and cities have understood the Holy Quran and lived with it as ordered by the Lord of the Worlds, many of whom have had their lives to serve Islam.

I believe that after the era of the rightly-guided Caliphs, that some of those who conveyed the meanings of religion to us, in good faith, have resorted to the traditional style of preaching (da'wah to Islam), and they delved into the interpretation of metaphysical issues in unconvincing ways to guide young people to Islam. Such as strictness in the provisions of the religion to the point of atonement, protecting a Muslim by mascot envelopes, the idea of torturing the dead in his grave with fire, that music is forbidden for us Muslims then this life is a life of misery, that women are lacking in brain and religion, women should be covered in black and their location is at home, a man can marry four women without conditions, and many more. All those wrong information are given before delving into an understanding of reality and material facts.

So the young man came to believe that he is a playground of the destiny of God Almighty and was powerless, while our God in the Qur'an tells us that every Self is held hostage to what it has done and that the human being is honored and God's successor on earth. God asks us to work so that God and His Messenger see our work. Human is responsible for his work and is rewarded with it in this world and the hereafter.

But, **unfortunately, the goals of Islamic religion have been misunderstood, and some Muslims became dependent, leaving life development, work, and the research in the roots of knowledge,** and surrendered their affairs to fate. Often when the truth is blind, it is a danger to human beliefs.

So we see some old yellow books are dry, devoid of the spirit of the worldly life and looking only at spirituality, its facts are blind, they exaggerated the inviolable and prohibitions, and added what they entrusted in their closed society, or what dictated to them customs and traditions. Therefore, they did not realize the true meanings of the Quran in that God revealed the Qur'an as guidance for people, **to make people happy in this world as in the hereafter**, to organize the good and loving relations between all his Muslim, infidel, animal, plant and inanimate creatures.

In our present world, we think and deal with systems, scales, and dimensions specific to our world; a Day represents the rotation of the Earth around itself, but will the earth rotate in paradise? a Meter has an agreed length in the world, and the Size is measured in three dimensions: length, width, height, and to locate a point we deal with four dimensions, which are length, width, height, and time, so we must manage and adhere to what we are asked in our real world. As for the occultism from the Holy Qur'an and some of the hadiths of the Messenger, they may have other systems and dimensions that we cannot visualize, so it is difficult for us to perceive them, but we accept their thoughts as they are.

For example, Allah said:

"Allah is the light of heaven and the earth... "(Alnoor 35)

"Be quick in the race..... And for gardens whose width is that of heavens and the earth prepared for the righteous" (Al Imran 133).

"Those who reject our signs ...As often as their skins are roasted through; We shall change them for fresh skins...." (Anisa' 56).

"... Their light will run forward before them and their right hands ..." (Altahreem 8).

"I do call to what ye see, and what you see not" (Alhaqa 38,39"

"......on a Day, space whereof will be as a thousand years of your reckoning" (Sajda/5)

"....Then we send her our angel and he appeared before her as a man in all respects" (Marya/17)

"So, and we shall join them to fair women with beautiful, big, and lustrous eyes" (Dhukhan/ 54).

Here we have to accept it as we received it without frills, and without comparing what is in our existing world.

# 15

## DOCTRINE OF REALITY

After what the Islamic conquests were spread in the East and West, and building the Umayyad and the Abbasid state, Muslims failed to communicate with the thoughts of the Qur'an and develop their meanings in proportion to the development of the human understanding of life. The Holy Qur'an is a clear Arabic language that calls for good morals, but away from bad morals, and calls for respect for others, even animal welfare. A believer does not need an excessive preach in asceticism, chastity, and intimidation of death and fire. **The believer loves God and God loves the believer, the believer humbled in front of God, he is not afraid of death, because he will be in the hands of his creator, and leaves fear of fire to the unbeliever.**

Since the distinguished Scholars of Islam began to interpret the Holy Quran to clarify the words of Allah, and to indicate what is meant for the people, some of these interpretations where differed somewhat according to the opinions of those scholars and according to their era, places, specialties, and interests, but the constants of religion remain clear. The reason is that the Arabic language of the Qur'an, although that Arabic language is clear, it is a broad language, and its phrases sometimes have many, but inconsistent, meanings. It is from this saying our master Ali, may God be pleased with him: "The Qur'an is a porter with faces."

In every era and sect, interpreters discovered some more understandable interpretations of their people. Therefore, **all interpretations of the Qur'an are correct, but they do not replace the Qur'an**. The Qur'an is the only source of Islamic legislation in every age and time, and it should be taken by a group of Muslim scholars of that era or people. God said:

"Nor should the Believers all go forth together: if a contingent from every expedition remained behind, they could devote themselves to studies in religion, and admonish the people when they return to them, that thus they may learn to guard themselves." (Altaubah 122).

But unfortunately, many of the books published in the modern era continued to convey what was interpreted in an ancient era and valid only for that era, as it is without careful consideration, and without understanding the doctrine of reality[3]. Then the Holy Qur'an is valid for every time and place if we understand its thoughts.

As an example: Our Sheikh Asha'rawy, may God have mercy on him, said that the transferring of human organs to other human is forbidden in Islam, perhaps for fear of being trafficked, but if you set limits, grounds, laws, and the advancement of modern science, the process becomes beneficial to humans and does not contradict religion.

In another example, God says in the holy verse 16 of Surat al-Nahal:

"And marks, and by the stars guide themselves"

The interpretations of the past time say that man was guided during his travels by the knowledge of the position of the stars. That is true, but in our time, does an Airplane pilot should know the stars to know his destination and altitude? Our earth is a Star, it has earth gravity, and around the earth is a magnetic field, so in navigation today a barometer is influenced by the gravity of the earth to give Airplane height, and there is a compass influenced by the magnetism of the Earth to guide the Airplane its direction.

Add to that the distorted hadiths of the innocence of true Islam. Al-Bukhari, may God rest his soul, has collected the hadiths of Our Lord Muhammad, but today I find books for Bukhari's hadiths which are suitable for Sunnis, others for Shiites, and many other editions!!

Therefore we see some of today's youth abandoning Islam, because of what is recited to them from what is unrealistic and attributed to Islam because it does not answer many of their questions, it does not match reality or logic. Like also "cutting the thief's hand, hitting the wife, the fire that burns the dead in his grave, stoning to death, the countries of the infidels beautiful, and the scourge adorer Muslims and much more non-realities interpretation of our holy Quran.

The modern man differs from his ancestors, he is a materialist who believes in the physical and doubts the occult. For that and to renew the call to Islam we have to clarify the merits of the Islamic religion in the existing life, God created the universe and laid down rules and laws for it to work and put us a catalog that shows us how we can live happily. God does not need us but we need God, God knows everything and we do not know everything. So many real believers have donated the right in our day to show the right values of Islam, despite opposing petrified minds.

I am sure that distinguished scholars of our time have touched on this issue to defend the correct Islam, but still, those who are confronted with frozen minds by searching for their missteps and not appreciating the correctness of their understanding, accusing them of heresy, and they relied on transmitted hadiths, far from the logic of the Holy Qur'an and reality.

I respect all the hadiths of Prophet Mohammad, but we cannot deduce from them a ruling unless this ruling is applied and applied in the time of our noble Messenger and is in line with the morals of the

Prophet Muhammad, peace be upon him, he was sent to fulfill the morals. So we have to be careful, then the transferred talk about several people, some words could be forgotten, misrepresented, or diminished from it a word or a letter, and it will lose its original meaning, and it can be considered heritage or a good disposition, and if the hadith is correct, I will not be held accountable as a sin and go to hell, because entering Hellfire is subject to the day of reckoning.

Also, I believe that we cannot deduce from the hadith a new ruling on religion, because the entire rulings of religion are present in the Holy Qur'an and their interpretation is clear from the authentic hadiths.

As for the hadith seen with the eye, man can remember it, and if it is narrated it becomes audible. Any hadith which practically applied, understood and knows how, and knows its significance, such as prayer and rituals in Hajj, fasting, zakat, righteousness with parents, respect for the neighbor, and many other correct ones, and then we apply what almighty God saying:

"What the messenger brought to you, take it, and what he forbids you about, so finish"

# 16

## PHILOSOPHY OF RECYCLING

God has created various benefits in life from the principle of Recycling, God says:

"...And there are those who bury gold and silver and spend it not in the way of Allah: announce unto them a most grievous penalty" (Altaobah 34)

It is supposed that gold, silver, and money should not be stockpiled, but should go spinning and moving from one man to another, so to be used in industry, agriculture, and trade and creating profit for people; for the owner and the workers those who work with. That is, money must always be mobile to increase its value by adding work, so we benefit and also pay its zakat. Money value is reduced with time, and perhaps also gold and silver. Recycle Money in work and trade is a principle imposed by Islam.

God says:

"By no means have ye attained righteousness unless ye give freely of that which ye love..." (Alemran 92)

"He that doeth good shall have ten times as much to his credit…" (Alana'am 160).

Well, when you spend zakat from what you like or do a good job, it's benefit will come back to you and you gain more, then you spend, then you gain, then you spend, then you gain, etc… And so recycled…

God said also:

"Seest thou not that Allah makes the clouds move gently, and then joins them together, and then makes them into a heap? – then wilt thou see rain issue forth from their midst and He sends down from the sky mountain masses of clouds wherein hail…" (Alnoor 43).

The seawater in its Cycle evaporates and becomes a cloud, then it descends on the mountains as rain, and it will flow through valleys, watering the plantings and creatures. Water then return to the sea then goes Cycle again, after it has benefited what God created on this earth.

As for the Temperature of lightning in the sky, which is the result of static electricity when clouds rub each other, this will reach 6,000 °C, this high Temperature produces Nitric acid from Nitrogen and oxygen in the air, which turns into nitrate fertilizers when it contacts the soil and feeds the plants from which green chlorophyll is made. The chlorophyll in turn decomposes and produces Nitrogen and Oxygen that nourish the air. Plants grow, reproduce, and bear fruits, then die and decompose, to be fertilizers. And so on Cycles of water, Nitrogen, Oxygen, and Plants continue.

Many other examples and verses in the Quran speak of the **principle of Recycling, which is one of the reasons for the continuity of this life in which we live.**

Since Adam was created by God, and deposited in his chromosomes the instinct or common sense and the Clairvoyance, that is passed on from generation to generation, we are born, grow up, then we put our chromosomes in our children and we die. Thus God created life from the principle of Recycling.

The lie or lack of faith that people believe in, that the land resources are limited and not sufficient to increase the population. Didn't God say; "There is no moving creature on earth but its sustenance dependeth on Allah: He knoweth the time and place of its definite abode and its temporary deposit: all is in a clear Record" (Hud 6).

If we take the principle of recycling, it will be more than enough in the land. God has given us the vision to create and gave us the strength to do. There are still a lot of creative ideas, including the principle of recycling, and the exploitation of what is in our hands, such as hydroponic cultivation and others. The capacity of our insights and our ability to think is unlimited. God has set no restrictions or limits for our minds to take from his knowledge. We still need a lot of development in this life and work. We always have to think about the abundance of resources in the land, look for it, and recycle it.

It is also a principle of recycling; that God created opposites in humans and animals so that life could continue. Creating a strong against a strong one to kill him so that a weak can live, then the weak become strong and kills another strong or perishes this strong from within, and thus life continues. God created a whale to eat fish and fish eat planktons, plankton later eats the whale.

Praise you, My Lord, how great you are.

# 17

## KNEED & DESIRE

Sometimes we say: This is God's will and desire. But where are man's will and desire?

God has the greatest will, and man represents the smallest wish.

What is the nature of the relationship between men's will and desire? Is it manageable???

Many philosophers have touched on this subject, even to the faiths and religions. The pessimistic German philosopher Arthur Schopenhauer[9] defines the desire that it is born of needs, deprivation, and suffering, which are the truth of humans and his essence because it is linked to the characteristic of his consciousness. Because, it is a lust accompanied by consciousness, which is awareness of what he desires, wants, and seeks to through his will, it is the effort that the soul makes to satisfy its desire to preserve itself.

**But the human will not satisfy all his desires, once he has satisfied a desire until it generates a new desire**, he begins to seek and constantly search for the realization of the new desire, which makes man never rest, and the possibility of obtaining happiness becomes impossible. That is in the opinion of some philosophers.

But, I believe that it is necessary to distinguish between negative desire and positive desire. People are different; every human being has definite percentages of these five elements: **intelligence**, **ambition**, material, and moral **possibilities**, ability to **endure,** and patience, in addition to his **personality** components for reaching his goal. Then for a person to be successful in reaching what he wishes, and to be a positive one, It is essential that the ratios for each of all above-mentioned elements should be positive (>60%):

a) **A positive desire**: when combined with ambition and possibilities, it is real, precisely defined, reasonable, and doable, with right endure and personality. It leads its person to success and happiness.

b) **A Negative desire**: when combined with ambition only, it is the hope, is usually in the imagination, undefined, without or low possibilities, it is unreasonable, either because of the lack of tools, lack of intelligence, and non-endure, or a shaky personality. The person became in constant torment.

Therefore a person must know his abilities and potentials. It is dangerous when the will alone control the body and the mind, to carry out desires. Where it creates false justifications to reach the realization of desires, here the body is used for will purposes, then the body aging and fray, but the will does not age, and ends with the death of the human.

Therefore, some philosophical, Buddhist, and Christian doctrines found to escape the torment caused by the desire of man to kill desire or even to kill themself. For example, a lover kills himself if he does not win the love of his beloved, and some Christian priests kill the lust for sex so that they do not marry, as well as the devout Buddhist.

But Islam Religion did not ask to kill human desire; Islam rather found a better way to adapt and managing it with controls to create a better life.

God Messenger Prophet Mohammad said to three Muslims, who wanted abstinence in life and devoting their time to prayer and worship only:

"Are you who said so and so? As for me, I fear God more than you, and I am more pious than you, but I fast and break my fast, pray, rest, and marry women, whoever rejects my style is not my follower."

Then desires are at numerous levels of liabilities [10], whether physical, humaneness, or divine. Islam has set the highest standards and rejected destructive and despicable levels. Islam respected the human body and its desires and considered the body the means to enter paradise or fire. So Islam imposed the satisfaction of the body and its desires from the higher levels of chastity and rejected the levels of villains.

God reminds us in the Holy Qur'an that most of the members of the human body such as hands, heart, tongue, and skin will witness us on the day of Resurrection, so they are beings connected to our body and act on the orders of our mind, the executive director of the soul in our body. They are beings, some of which are directly mocked by the normal human being to be controlled such as hands, legs, and the eye. The other is involuntary control, which can be also voluntary controlled by strengthening the will and positive desires if we are trained to do so.

God has created the law of will, i.e. the possibility of controlling our behavior, actions, and instincts, and taking control of some involuntary organs such as pain and even slowing down blood circulation.

If we can, with our conscious mind, control our desires and upgrade them and practice controlling our will, we can make our lives happy. Training exercises to strengthen the will may be difficult or difficult, they are similar to exercises used to strengthen the muscles of our body, because those exercises may stress the person psychologically, but the results are good, they will enable you to reject temptations and harmful pleasures.

For example: **Focus in prayer**: in a quiet and secluded place, if we focus in our prayers after saying

"Allahu Akbar", we should leave all thoughts of our world, and realize that we are now in presence of our Creator, talking to him and confirm that God is before us hearing us. Then we may have started the first lesson in adjusting our thoughts and our organs. I know it's one of the hardest things because the ideas and things of our world which pass in our minds per minute could be over fifty ideas!!! We will get rid of them by focusing on and practicing.

Also **fasting Ramadan**: it is annual training for refining the desires of the Body and the Self, such as speech, anger, and sex, because fasting is not only about food.

**Meditate 20 minutes a day:** sit outdoor or indoor and focus on your breathing (inspiration/exhalation) the mind is trained to focus, and its results are amazing [46].

Another example: **How to expel insomnia:** and kick out thoughts from your mind to sleep? Lie in your bed and focus your thinking on relaxing the first big toe of your right foot, then go to the index toe, be sure it's relaxed, take your time, then to the middle toe, then to the fourth toe, then to the little toe, then and repeat it to the left foot … and so on the hands' fingers and other body organs… until you make sure that it is rested take your time.

Surely you will sleep and you don't know where you stopped relaxation exercise.

It is a way to focus your thoughts on one subject...

# 18

## KNEED & HABITS

What is a habit?? The habit is a behavior we repeat it many times, it is difficult to do it at the beginning because we need an effort to convince our perception of its work, and then it becomes easy because our brain liked it and considered it axiomatic, to reduce the necessary energy for its.

The human brain is a super-developed computer, if we commit to repeating a certain behavior our brain converts it into a nervous adaptation, and then it will become a habit, and becomes done in an orderly and continuous manner and without a thoughtful effort.

For example, a baby, when he stands up for the first time it's hard for him, then he walks and run and his thoughts are busy with something else.

If it wasn't for habits, we wouldn't be able to work, move, and think about many things at the same time.

The energy needed at the beginning to acquire a habit is usually influenced by effort and internal factors from the human being and from outside his body. Will is one of these factors, as well as the companions, the community, and time is other factors.

Some habits are good and some are bad... Good habits are the ones that create a successful human being, and bad habits destroy him. Unfortunately, it's easy to get a bad habit because at first you don't need a lot of effort and you see its tempting results immediately, such as smoking a cigarette or drinking alcohol. While a good habit initially needs more effort and results appear after days or weeks, such as reading books habit or gymnastic exercises.

Getting rid of bad habits also needs a great effort, because getting rid of it needs to stay away from the usual comrades as it needs also a strong will to neglect the observations around you from some people, and not to be weak in the face of its temptations and incentives.

The Messenger of God (pbuh) said:

"He who searches for good is given to him, and who protects himself from evil is protected from it".

In other words, habits are from the will, weak wills cannot control habit, while strong Wills can control habits. The Willpower of man helps him to organize his life and contributes greatly to his success in both study and work [11]. As well as, maintaining his health and staying away from anything harmful to him. Willpower is like any other muscle in the human body, improving and strengthening it by training, so God has prescribed fasting in Ramadan as well as prayer. God said:

"O, ye who believe! Fasting is prescribed to you as it was prescribed to those before you....Fasting for a fixed number of days....And it is better for you that ye fast if ye only knew" (Albaqara 183,184)

At an American university[12] in 1972, the Marshmallow Test was conducted on a group of children whose activities and progress in life were followed for 20 years."

At first, the children were placed in front of pieces of candy and asked every child not to eat his candy until he is authorized. Those who adhered to the instructions would be rewarded with another candy piece, and if they ate them before he was authorized, he would not be rewarded another piece. These experiences continued for a while. Years later they found that those who were the most patient became more successful in their lives.

Fasting Ramadan is for God and God rewards us in this world before the hereafter. One of its advantages is to train the will of humans to be patient on hunger, thirst, desires, and patience when hurt.

Prophet Mohammad said:

"Fasting is half the patience," he said also: "Fasting the month of patience and three days....."

Weak-willed People cannot get rid of bad habits if they have them, and they often complain about their miserable condition, even if it is better than others, they become unhappy with self-intimation. **Thus, when a**

**weak will hears a negative comment from someone else, he is quickly influenced, because of the lack of self-confidence.**

Many studies and books look at acquiring good habits that help us succeed in our work and happiness in our lives, for example:

1- We should set priorities; important, not important, urgent, not urgent.
2- To focus on our target, target should be always in our mind.
3- We should cooperate with others and be proactive.
4- We should find our deficiencies and fix them immediately.
5- A good communication if you listen to others and let others understands you.
6- You win when others win.

# 19

## GLANDS ARE BODY INSTRUMENTS

God has forbidden man to eat pork for reasons that only Allah knows, God said:

"He hath only forbidden you dead meat, blood, the flesh of swine, and that on which any other name hath been invoked besides that of Allah. But if one is forced by necessity, without willful disobedience, nor transgressing due limits, then he guiltless. For Allah is Oft-Forgiving, Most Merciful" (Alana'am 115).

If we look at the composition of the biological pig, which is similar to the human formation, we will find that its hormones [19, 18] are mostly identical to those of humans. So drug development companies try their new drugs on pigs before giving them to humans to make sure that these drugs are effective.

In the human body, there are more than fifty Glands and endocrine glands that produce enzymes and hormones manufactured in glands created by God within our bodies. These glands secrete precisely specific amounts of each hormone that goes to the stomach or to the bloodstream that connects it to the area designated for each hormone to activate the organ or stop its activity by a certain percentage. It means that our hormones (Body's Chemical Messengers) are the micro-devices (Instrument Control) that control us. They control the management of all activities of our body system. Control reproduction and growth, control the growth of our organs, diseases, health, and many more, and even our activity, mood, desires, and everything.

For example, the Pepsin Enzyme in the mouth, which breaks the protein into amino acids, and the Thyroid hormone where it's idle, cause fatigue and feeling of cold, and weight increase. The pituitary gland is considered to be responsible for human size, length, and maturing. The lymphatic gland is responsible for the resistance of the germs, and the pineal gland is responsible for changing psychological state in humans, and for the regulation of time, for the sexual condition and type, as the estrogen hormone that controls the female condition and homosexuality, its side effect can lead to schizophrenia effects [47], and so on...

After careful examinations, the doctor usually gives the patient a certain hormone with a definite concentration depending on the condition of the gland and its secretion, for example, the Thromycin is given in case of hypothyroidism.

If we eat pork, its hormones, which is, as I mentioned, close to human hormones, these are chemicals, are transferred to our blood, and some of our hormones increase, which will make imbalance, that will affect our organs, mood, or behavior, or so-called Hormonal Disorder.

# 20

## CLAY RACE

The Qur'an has indicated that Allah created Our Lord Adam from clay, God said:

"Behold! Thy Lord said to the angels:" I am about to create man, from mire molded clay into shape; When I have fashioned him in due proportion, and breathed into him of My spirit, fall ye down in obeisance unto him" (Alhijr 28, 29)

The mire molded clay is black dry clay with a sharp scent; scientifically a mixture of oxides, hydroxides, and mineral salts such as calcium, phosphorus, silica, iron, etc. and the smell is caused by the presence of organic hydrocarbons.

God also said:

"Man we did create from a strain of clay" (Almo'menoon 12).

God then explains with scientific accuracy how the embryo that feeds on the mother's blood is formed and therefore the mother's blood comes from the food that is originally from what the clay land grows.

The clay strain consists of different elements and sequences in its status relative to the number of protons in the nucleus, and our Lord here left us to research and reflect on it, the strain is when we say that hydrogen has one proton and helium has two protons and lithium has three and beryllium has four, etc... and so carbon, nitrogen, oxygen ... 6، 7، 8، ... each element atom is distinguished from that before in the series of rotating elements by increasing one proton. This is what the Russian scientist Mendeleev discovered and set the periodic ranking table of the elements from which God created everything in our world: (from a strain of clay).

All plants grow up from clay, then animals eat plants, and humans eat plants and animals. By the power of God, and in a preserved position within the human body the sperm is formed, then it turns into a leech, then an embryo, then bone, then the bones are coated with flesh. Then a sane living human, full of spirit and insight and in the most beautiful form, consisting of carbon, hydrogen, nitrogen, calcium, sodium, iron, carbon, and oxygen. Bless be God, He is the best Creator.

Thus, God describes his creation to the human race in a delightful detail that man did not reach until hundreds of years after the Qur'an came down on our Profit Muhammad (PUH). This undermines the so-called Darwin theory [35] which claims that all living organisms come from common ancestors, and then differ into a tree of factions and species as a result of different conditions and environments. But God created man from clay, God also created other creatures such as animals and monkeys, but he did not blow them out of his soul and did not give them the clairvoyance as humans (otherwise to mention it in the Qur'an), but God granted those creatures Self, personality and Instinct.

# 21

## SLAVERY & RELIGION

Throughout the ages, the sources of slavery have been and continue to be many. Qur'an text says equality among mankind. Its principles call for justice and equality among human beings, and these principles are incompatible with having another human being as a slave. What is permissible is slavery for God alone or the worship of God.

But one of the morals accepted by the Arabs and the world before Islam was that in wars prisoners were exploited as slaves, so God put in his law various ways of freeing prisoners and slaves.

The honorable Prophet Mohammad came to complete the honors of morality, not to produce a revolution that would be rejected by the Arabs then. Firstly he prescribed to the captive that if he became a Muslim or teaches Muslim writing he becomes free. That is to stop bloodshed and respect for the captured as a human being, God created the prisoner even if he is not a Muslim, we have to feed him with what we eat and give him clothing with what we wear until the war ends.

Islam legalized emancipation and did not legalize slavery, as it is prescribed for each penance the liberation of a slave, then whoever has a maid slave and did not want to free her; he is allowed to marry her so that she would be fully entitled to full rights as a wife.

**It was therefore assumed that after a generation of Muslims had passed, there would be no bondage to a human being.**

God said:

"O mankind! We created you from a single pair of a male and a female, and made you into nations and tribes, that ye may know each other. Verily the most honored of you in the sight of Allah, he who is the most righteous of you, and Allah has full knowledge and is well acquainted" (Alhujurat 13)

God said:

"But he hath made no haste on the path that is steep. And what will explain to thee the path that steep? It is freeing the bondman" (Albalad 11-13).

Unfortunately, some of those who claim to be religious did not understand this logic, we find that slavery continued and did not free slaves, even 1,300 years after the descent of the heavenly message. We find, for example, a market for the possession of slaves in Yemen in the 13th century, and the trafficking of slaves in Yemen and other areas around it continued to the nineteenth century. We also find in the notices of the traveler ibn Khaldun's Foremost during his travels

[26], whenever he passes through an Islamic country, the Sultan granted him a maid to enjoy and leave it. Also during the reign of Hmmoud ibn Muhammad (who claims to Islam) Sultan Zanzibar (1896-1902) dealing with human trafficking, till he complied with the British colonizer's demands prohibiting human trafficking, and many others. What Islam is that?

Human freedom came from Qur'an 1450 years ago, but today in the age of atoms and world civilization, slavery has evolved in all countries of the world except the few and has become a kind of business and with legal licenses:

1) The bondage of the possession of one human being to another, such as human trafficking and the appropriation of villages with its people.

2) Bondage of the job with contracts such as the sale of a ballplayer, or the control of a country by society or other countries after being flooded with debt.

3) The bondage of thought, so that a state, a human being, a doctrine allows the enslavement of another human being by force or oppression with certain ideas and actions.

God said:

"Let there be no compulsion in religion; Truth stands out clear from Error: ….".(Albaqara 256)

# 22

## EARTH SWERVES & WEATHER CHANGES

The following Quranic verses surprised me: in the name of God, the most merciful and merciful:

"Do not the unbelievers see that the heavens and the earth were joined together as one unit of creation before We clove them asunder? We made from water every living thing, will they not then believe? And We have set on the earth mountains standing firm, lest it should shake with them, and We have made therein broad highways for them to pass through: that they may receive Guidance. And We have made the heavens as a canopy well-guarded: yet do they turn away from the signs which these things... It is He Who created the Night and the Day, and the sun and the moon: all swim along, each in its Orbital" (AlAnbyaa' 31-33).

Hallelujah, here are five scientific miracles in eight lines. This leads us to scientific thoughts and opinions in these verses:

(1) **The Heavens**: The explosion of the great universe and the creation of the Earth, means

that the whole universe was bound like a fist and then extended by God to be the earth, planets, and stars and still expanding... God said:

"And We who construct the Firmament with power and skill, and We Who Broadens". (Altharyat 47)

Based on previous scientific theories and research from Einstein, Newton, J.Kepler and modern Palmer Laboratories [27, 28], the diameter of the universe has become 93 billion light-years and is still expanding as a result of **centrifugal forces**. The location of each celestial object depends on its mass and the speed of its rotation.

But the mass decreases with time and leads to a reduction in the speed of its rotation, this weakens the strength of the centrifugal force.

Then our God goes on to tell us the end of this world and to assure us of his oneness:

"To Allah do belongs the unseen of the heavens and the earth, and to Him goeth back every affair..." (Hood 123)

That is, this universe, which is of god's command, will eventually return to God and disappear.

In another verse, God explains to us how heaven and planets will turn to him. Where there will be **attraction forces** to planets and stars, when the influence of centrifugal forces ends or subsides, gravity overcomes and becomes very powerful so that it attracts everything even the light. And God tells us that the universe will return as its first beginning:

"The Day that we roll up the heavens like a scroll rolled up for books, even as We produced the first creation, so shall We produced a new one: a promise We have undertaken: truly shall We fulfill it" (Alanbyaa' 104).

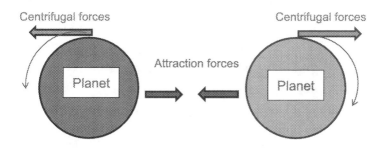

(2) **The Water:** Biologists disagreed [31] on where the living cell was starting to be, but most of them - and based on fossil microbial research - proved that the basis of life began from water 3.5 billion years ago, millions of years ago before God created Our Master Adam. As the water in the oceans is for the durability of life, without water the sun would burn the earth and what is on it in an instant. Because the specific heat of water is much higher than rocks and solid material. Seawater stores heat from the sun in the daytime without being hot enough and release it at night. Besides that seawater evaporates to be clouds and the clouds rubbing each other and release high voltage of static electricity which produces lightning,

and converts oxygen and nitrogen air into the nitrates that melt in the rainwater and be a nitrogen fertilizer for the plant, creating life on earth. As explained in this book, the subject of recycling principle.

(3) **Earth shaking:** also check God's words: "And We have set on the earth mountains standing firm, lest it should shake with them". This means that God constantly and very accurately makes the earth balanced so as not to sway and shake and perish its inhabitants. Imagine if your car wheel is unbalanced and you drive at a speed of 50 kilometers/hour, what happens to the car? Of course, the car will shake, and the more speed, the more you annoy the passengers. The balance of the earth that rotates itself at 1660 km/h (If we divide the earth's circumference by the hours of the day, we get: $= 40000/24$) (i.e. three times faster than an Airplane), but we, its inhabitants, do not feel any vibration because God continuously adjusts its balance so as not to shake.

The reason for the change in the earth's climate, or more precisely, is the displacement of the four seasons every few years, not only the carbon dioxide emitted by factories and cars- the formation of the so-called glass house and the heating of the earth's surface- but also because of melting huge mountains of snow in the poles. Mountains of snow have been removed from its position, and now what happens when some of the Snowy Mountains melted?

(a) Over the past years, the center of the poles has been shifted to maintain the balance of the earth [29], i.e. the movement of the axis of rotation of the earth somewhat, and thus shifting of the orbits; the Capricorn, the Cancer, and the Equator little by little, so that spring overlaps summer, summer overlaps winter, and winter overlaps spring. In another theory for the reason for the displacement of the center of the North and South Pole is that the huge and molten iron mass in the center of the Earth, moves slowly every few years, i.e. the earth's magnets are shifted a little from their place and then return.

(b) Let's also think about the melted snow water. Where it goes? Of course to the sea, and therefore raise the sea level even millimeters slower every year!! Then it covers part of the land!! Consider what God Almighty said:

"See they not that We gradually reduce the land from its outlying borders?" (Alra'ad 41).

(4) **<u>Canopy Heavens:</u>** In the supplement of the above verses, our Lord reminds us that sky is

109

preserved over the earth, or rather a keeper of the earth and those in it!: "And We have made the heavens as a canopy well-guarded" How?

The earth is a massive magnet, and the magnetic field around it in the sky saves it from deadly Solar wind such as X and Gama rays.

(5) **Planet Orbits:** The Sun, the Moon, and the earth rotate each in its Orbit, and do not interfere with the other. The word swimming here means that they move because of the forces of their own, from within them [30]. The elders thought that the earth is flat, Sun and Moon move in a circle around. We now know that earth is rounded.

# 23

## PHARAOHS MADE CEMENT

Building the pyramids...

- When I went for hajj in 2011, I was reading the Qur'an in Arafat tent, young Iraqis sat down near me and said: Increase our knowledge O Sheikh (I was bearded). I said I am neither a sheikh nor a scholar of religion, but come and let us mediate some verses of Qur'an; I opened the Qur'an book and read:

"O, Haman! Light fire on the clay, and build for me a structure."(Alqasas 38).

Since I am a chemical engineer, I remembered:

1 -   The Romans built their houses and castles, which exists till now, from volcanic ash.
2 -   Mineral carbonate of calcium, iron, magnesium, aluminum, and chromium, when heated above the temperature of 1,000 °C, loses carbon dioxide and turns into oxides.
3 -   When mixing those oxides with water and placing them in molds, the lost carbon dioxide

is restored over time from that dissolved in water and from the atmosphere and the molded material returns to its origin as a stone, i.e. cement.

4 - The word "fire" in the Qur'an verse, does not mean heat up, or warm, or hot, it means to make fire with Temperature over 1000°C.

5 - This is how cement factories manufacture different types of cement according to the clay components used.

6 - The pyramids do not contain fossils or veins; as volcanic stones, they are not from quarries or volcanic rocks.

That means that The Pharaoh of Egypt was asking the architect of the building Haman to light a fire under the clay stones to turn it into oxides to make construction cement, just as we today make the construction material and cement material. So God tells us how Pharaohs build the Pyramids.

# 24

## ECONOMY IN LIVING

To rejoice in God's many blessings upon us is a nice thing, likewise, from what is permissible, we have to enjoy the adornment of life that God brought to His servants and the goodness of sustenance. God said:

"Say: Who hath forbidden the beautiful gifts of Allah, which He hath produced for his servants, and the things, clean and pure, which He hath provided for sustenance? Say they are, in the life of this world, for those who believe and purely for them on the Day of Judgment...." (Ala'araf 32).

But one of the worst and ugliest habits is to waste what God has bestowed on us, such as strutting a suit, a new dress, or a fancy car to make those around us feel that we have something better than them, or exaggerating in food invitations, to inform the guest that we have more money under the pretext of honoring the guest. That is false generosity, also overeating, drinking, furniture, and dressing. These habits bring us a range of problems, especially health, psychological,

Dr. Eng. Fahim Jauhary

and social, as well as material problems. They are causes of illness, cancer, envy, and anger of others.

Ramadan is between the manifestations of generosity and the scourge of extravagance that is denied in Islam: in the Holy Qur'an about 23 times, Allah almighty forbids us from extravagance in his grace.

God said:

"...But waste not by excess: for Allah loveth not the wasters" (Alana'am 141)

"...eat and drink: But waste not by excess, for Allah, loveth not the wasters" (Ala'raf 31)

"...and the Transgressors will be Companions of the fire!" (Ghafer 43)

"And follow not the bidding of those who are extravagant. Who make mischief in the land, and mend not their ways." (Alshua'ara 151,152)

"Those who, when they spend, are not extravagant and not niggardly, but hold a just balance between those extremes" Alfurqan 67).

Ramadan month is not a month of waste and pleasure of having many bounties and food for its owner, as some radios and TV stations sought and belie, but it is a month of giving for the poor, a month of patience and strengthening the Will of the Muslim.

# REFERENCES

1) Holy Qur'an

2) تاريخ فلاسفة ألإسلام لإبن رشد.
   (History of the philosophers of Islam by Ibn Rushed)

3) فقه الواقع وأثره في الإجتهاد، د.ماهر حصوه، جامعة العين..
   (Jurisprudence of reality & its impact on diligence, Dr. Maher Haswa)

4) كتابة بسيم مسالمة – آخر تحديث: مارس, 2017.
   (Baseem Salmeh Book, March 2017)

5) Mined structures, Annemieke Cloosterman, Netherlands..

6) Dr. Ibrahim Alfiky,

7) Newton's Law of Gravity between Masses.

8) ألمهاتما غاندي.
   (Mahatma Gandhi)

9) The School of Life, Arthur Schopenhauer

10) د. مصطفى محمود، كيفية تناول الإسلام ألإرادة والرغبة..
    (How Islam deals with will & desire, Dr. Mustafa Mahmoud)

11) Think & Grow Rich, Napoleon Hill

12) The Marshmallow Test, Prf. W. Michel, Stanford University,

13) The Power of your subconscious Mind, Dr. J. Murphy 1898-1981, CA, USA

14) قوة العقل الباطن، د. إبراهيم الفقيه..
    (The power of the subconscious mind, Dr. Ibrahim Al-Fakih)

15) Most Interesting Ideas of S. Freud, By Saul McLeod, 2018.

16) كتاب القضاء والقدر، محمد متولي الشعراوي، دار الشروق..
    (The book of Judiciary & Destiny, Dr. Mahmoud Metwally Shaarawi)

17) Human Nature & the State, H. S. Brown, International Journal of Ethics.

18) Pigs are biologically similar to humans and are thus frequently used for human medical research/ en.wikipedia.org.

19) Porcine Somatotropin (pST), Bio-technology Information Series

20) ..المهندس عدنان الرفاعي –المعجزة الكبرى
(The Great Miracle, Eng. Adnan Al-Rifai)

21) ..ألكتاب والقرآن، د.م.محمد شحرور
(The Book & The Qur'an, Dr.Eng. Muhammad Shahrour)

22) Why Brain need much Energy, N. Swaminathan, USA 2008

23) Dr. Surjit Safilyaf, Russian Science Academy of Nerves,.

24) Emotional Intelligence, PhD. Steven J. Stein.

25) ..خواطر شعراوي، العلم السماوي والعلم الكوني، يوتيوب
(Celestial science & cosmic science, thought of Dr. M. Shaarawi)

26) ..مقدمة إبن خلدون، عبد الرحمن بن محمد بن خلدون
(Ibn Khaldun Introduction, by Abdul Rahman M. Ibn Khaldun)

27) The Gravitational Instability of the Universe, NASA, by PJE Palmer, 1967.

28) A Brief History of Time, Stephen Hawking,

29) National Geographic, 2016/04, North Pole Displacement.

30) Dr. Maurice Bacilli, The Bible the Quran and the Science

31) The Secret of how Life on Earth Began, Michael Marshall, 2016.

32) ..قاموس المعاني- عربي/ عربي
(Meanings Dictionary, Arabic/Arabic)

33) Scientific Study published in 1907 by Duncan MacDougall, Massachusetts.

34) Religious views of Isaac Newton – Wikipedia.

35) Charles Darwin, The Descent of Man, and Selection in relation to Sex, J. Tyler.

36) Proven Process for Success, Brian Tracy.

37) How I bought my dream House, John Assaraf.
38) The history of western Philosophy, Bertrand Russell.
39) Wisdom Bias & Balance, Ass. Prof. Igor Grossman, Waterloo Univ., Canada.
40) Wisdom from Phil, by Stephan S. Hall.
41) How to think like a wise Person, by Dr. Adam Grant.
42) 10 Ways to think like a wise Person.
43) Stanford Encyclopedia, Wisdom, Jan. 8th.2007.
44) George Wilhelm F. Hegel, Wikiquote.
45) Abdullah Quilliam, April 1856, Int.
46) The Incredible Benefits of Meditation on your willpower, Colin Robertson, 2015.
47) A role for Estrogen in Schizophrenia, A. Gogos, A. Shisa & B. Dean, International Journal of Endocrinology.

Printed in the United States
By Bookmasters